OUTRAGEOUS CONDUCT:
Bizarre Behavior At Work

N. Elizabeth Fried, Ph.D.

OUTRAGEOUS CONDUCT:
Bizarre Behavior At Work

N. Elizabeth Fried, Ph.D.

INTERMEDIARIES Press
Dublin, Ohio

Available directly from the Society for Human Resource Management
1-800-444-5006

For additional information, contact:

INTERMEDIARIES Press
5590 Dumfries Court West, Suite 2000
Dublin, OH 43017

10 9 8 7 6 5 4 3 2 1

Library of Congress Cataloging-in-Publications Data

Fried, N. Elizabeth.
    Outrageous conduct : bizarre behavior at work / N. Elizabeth
Fried.
        p. cm.
    ISBN 0-942361-41-5
    1. Personnel management—Humor. 2. Human behavior—Humor.
I. Title.
HF5549.F7445   1991   91-14020
658.3'00207—dc20   CIP

Cover illustration by Apai Pratoommas
Typography by The Production House

DEDICATION

*To all my secret sources for their confidence and trust,
with special affection for "J" who regaled me one afternoon
for nearly five hours with story, after story, after story.*

FOREWORD

This book evolved quite serendipitously. I was in Texas giving a presentation about salary administration to my client's board of directors. Since the board was not very sophisticated, the head of the organization instructed me to define everything I said.

"Let me tell you about our board, Elizabeth," he began. "You just can't tell this group that you went to the market to get pay data. When you say 'market,' they think it's a place to buy bananas."

With that in mind, I took great care to simplify my presentation. I slowly went through my slides and carefully explained how my firm developed the salary program. Everything went smoothly and the board accepted the plan. After I left, the board went into executive session, so several of the senior managers were excused from the meeting. As they filed into the hotel lobby, they saw me standing in line to check out. Several of the managers gathered around me to offer their congratulations on the effective presentation. Naturally, I was delighted that they were pleased.

A few managers, however, decided that they wanted to have some fun. The research manager started. "You know, Elizabeth, our board is so unsophisticated that we probably didn't need to pay you all this money to come down here."

"Yeah," the administrative manager chimed in, "with this group, we probably could've hired an actress and told them it was you. They never would've known the difference."

I just laughed and shook my head. "What a bunch of characters," I thought.

A moment later the bellman announced that my airport shuttle was ready to depart, so I said my "good-byes" and boarded the van. All I could think about during the entire drive out to the airport was that they were one of my nuttiest clients. Although they were one of my favorite clients, they were certainly the most outrageous!

"If only I had the time to write about them," I thought. "But even if I did, there wasn't enough material to fill an entire book." Just as I was prepared to dismiss the concept and open my folder to review an article I was writing on retention bonuses, a new idea emerged. "Wouldn't it be great if I could get a whole collection of bizarre employee stories. Every one of my buddies across the country must have a good story or two. What great fun and a marvelous way to offer myself comic relief in between the complex, technical consulting engagements I have on the horizon."

And so it began. To generate excitement about the project, I contacted everyone I knew and trusted throughout the country. I talked to human resources professionals, security officers, business owners, and attorneys. I told them about my idea and asked them if they would help me. Most did, and they were terrific. Although they didn't provide specific names, they explained the circumstances and relevant facts. I promised them that their stories would be sufficiently altered to protect the individuals and the companies involved. They signed a document agreeing that they would never discuss with anyone that they had told me the stories, and I agreed never to reveal my sources. Part of the arrangement was that they had to have direct experience with the incidents. I was not interested in "corporate legends." I had to be sure that these stories were based on actual circumstances, so I required all contributors to have personal involvement with their cases.

I began interviewing in January, 1990 and continued through April. I logged in untold hours of interviews and a ton of stories. I poured through pages of transcripts and summarized all the anecdotes into twelve categories, which later became my chapters. Finally, I selected about three dozen of the best episodes.

I started writing in June and was amazed at how fast the chapters flowed. Although the essence of each story is true, I had to change or invent company and individual names, titles, places, dates, and certain other details to protect everyone involved. Thus, any name I used throughout the chapters arose strictly from my imagination and was not intended to represent any actual person either living or dead. So, if you recognize a name, consider it pure coincidence.

As I was developing the book, my assistant Sylvia Stansell was invaluable. We discussed story approaches and she was my first critic. She made sure that there were no missing pieces and that each story flowed logically. This was a nice break from her usual routine of reviewing lengthy, dry documents or crunching numbers.

Next, my neighbor Marianne Simpson, a former New York stockbroker, gave each chapter a critical eye. She reviewed the "dailies" at the local pool during her daughter's swimming lessons, while I paced nervously, awaiting her commentary and suggested revisions.

When the chapters were complete, I identified another group of wonderful human resources, public relations, and legal professionals who voluntarily agreed to review and comment on the stories. Each contributor was assigned selected chapters and subsequently developed his or her remarks. The individual comments were merged with those of others who were assigned the same chapter to produce a combined panel opinion. The legal comments were handled differently. The employment law expert had such a good time with his first assignment that he generously offered to review the entire manuscript. I jumped at the offer and created a separate section for legal comments.

I can't express how much I value and appreciate the willingness, interest, and effort of the entire group. Also, I especially want to recognize Tom Greble, the employment law expert, who gave me more than I ever expected. His comments were not just good, they were outstanding!

Through the group's combined efforts, they dramatically expanded the scope of the book from "beach reading" to the realm of "teach reading." The result is entertainment with a purpose, learning through laughter. And for this added dimension, I must credit Susan Stautberg of MasterMedia. She recommended that I write an analysis at the end of each story. I resisted—afraid it would destroy my creative mind-set. However, I finally compromised by suggesting a panel-of-experts approach.

Susan was absolutely on target. The panel's practical guidance, interspersed with wit and humor, provides valuable insight for readers. The panel members offer suggestions that range from how to deal with employees whose larceny becomes legendary to a few whose sexual exploits do the same!

To keep your reading breezy, I requested that the panel members conserve their responses. Thus, they purposely focused on a few key issues and did not address all aspects of each case. So, when you navigate through the narratives, keep in mind that the opinions expressed by the panel and particularly, our employment law expert, are offered only as general suggestions and should not be construed in any way as formal or legal advice. It's also important to note that their comments represent their *personal* opinions and not necessarily the policies and practices of the companies they represent.

Before I introduce you to the panel members, I want to recognize two other key people who contributed to this project. Arlene Baker, my copy editor, is truly an unsung hero. She is not only a meticulous, technical professional but also a terrific friend. I presented Arlene with a near-impossible deadline, and she rose to the occasion, rearranging her highly-committed writing schedule and working weekends and nights to finish the job. I applaud her stamina and most of all appreciate her friendship. Finally, I'd like to recognize Apai Pratoommas, the talented artist whose cartoon cover design caught your eye. "Joke," as he is aptly nicknamed, cleverly captured the colorful characters living within the pages.

Now that I've credited all the contributors to this project, let me formally introduce the panel members and employment law expert.

PANEL MEMBERS

FRANK BOSSE

Frank Bosse is vice president of human resources for the Fireman's Fund Personal Insurance Division, located in San Rafael, California. He has over fifteen years' human resources experience in a variety of industries, including retail, insurance, and federal and state governments. Bosse received his undergraduate degree from the State University of New York at Buffalo and his master's degree in industrial and labor relations from The Ohio State University.

LISA L. HUNTER

Lisa Hunter is president of the Newport Consulting Group, Inc., North Tarrytown, New York. The Newport Consulting Group is a human resources consulting firm that specializes in organizational effectiveness and compensation. Hunter has over fifteen years' experience as a practitioner in the communications, manufacturing, and health care industries. She also has a particular interest in international human resources applications and has expanded her practice to address those areas. She received her undergraduate degree in industrial and labor relations from Cornell University.

CATHY PRATT

Cathy Pratt, Ph.D., is a professor of public relations in the School of Journalism at The Ohio State University in Columbus, Ohio. Prior to joining the OSU faculty, Pratt had ten years' experience working in public relations in New York, where she performed the full scope of public relations services. She has a national reputation for research and writing on business ethics and is frequently engaged to speak before business and professional groups on this topic. She received her doctorate degree in mass communications from Bowling Green State University.

PEG THOMS

Peg Thoms is the principal consultant of her own firm located in Columbus, Ohio, where she specializes in leadership and management development. She has over ten years' experience as a human resources practitioner in the insurance industry, where her responsibilities included training and development, compensation and benefits, and employee relations. Thoms received her undergraduate degree from The Ohio State University and her master's degree from Texas Woman's University. Currently, she is pursuing her doctorate degree in organizational behavior at The Ohio State University.

BRAD A. WAITE

Brad Waite is the director of employee relations at Consolidated Stores of Columbus. He has over ten years' human resources experience in the retail industry, with a strong focus on employee relations, training and development, and risk management. Waite received his undergraduate degree from Franklin University and a master's degree in business administration from Capital University.

ANONYMOUS

Two panel members whose contributions were invaluable go unnamed because their organizations requested anonymity. One of the individuals works in a prominent position for a major public sector organization, and the other functions as a human resources professional for a high-tech manufacturing company. I regret that I can't introduce them along with the others and publicly recognize their contributions, but I must honor their requests.

EMPLOYMENT LAW EXPERT

THOMAS C. GREBLE

Thomas C. Greble is a partner in the New York City-based law firm of Roberts & Finger. His practice consists primarily of counseling and representing employers in employment-related matters, labor relations, equal employment opportunity law, and related litigation. Greble has represented private and public employers in judicial and administrative proceedings in numerous jurisdictions throughout the nation. He has also lectured and written extensively on employment-related topics to professional and business organizations. He is the author of *Manager's Guide to Employment Law*.

Greble is a graduate of Villanova University and Fordham University School of Law, where he has served as an adjunct professor of law. Greble is currently an adjunct professor at The New York University, where he teaches a graduate course in the Management Institute entitled "Fair Employment Practices." He is admitted to practice in the United States Supreme Court, various United States Courts of Appeal, and the State of New York.

ROBERTS & FINGER

Roberts & Finger is a law firm with offices in New York City and Morristown, New Jersey. It counsels and represents management in the areas of equal employment opportunity law, employment law, labor relations, and civil litigation. The firm has successfully represented employers in employment law litigation at the trial and appellate levels and before federal and state administrative agencies in various jurisdictions across the country.

Roberts & Finger believes that in today's litigious society, the only prudent and cost-effective employee relations philosophy for management to adopt is one of prevention, not cure. Skilled and aggressive representation in bargaining litigation and arbitration is, of course, very important. However, the firm believes that it is equally important for management to adopt policies and to manage individual situations in a manner designed to minimize the risk of formal proceedings and to maximize management's prospects of prevailing in those cases where formal proceedings cannot be forestalled.

Consistent with this proactive philosophy, Roberts & Finger assists employers in formulating policies and procedures, develops and conducts appropriate training programs, performs employee relations audits to identify potential problem areas, and regularly counsels management regarding the appropriate handling of complex and often sensitive employee relations problems.

Elizabeth Fried
Dublin, Ohio
June, 1991

TABLE OF CONTENTS

1
STAIRWELL LOVERS AND DON JUANS

They can be found in every company—willing, loving liaisons whose physical desires cross all boundaries. Their employee status can range from janitor to chief executive officer. When passion is fired, any available private corner will do—stairs, parking lots, storerooms, elevators, or closets. Most pairs go undetected, and we never learn of their secret trysts. Some make critical mistakes that lead to investigation and discovery. When caught, these highly inflamed lovers usually aren't fired. The embarrassment of their discovery typically does the trick.

THE CISCO KID

Cisco, the lead machinist on the floor, always fancied himself a ladies man. Whenever a woman would walk in the shop, he would flash a smile and, with unquestionable sincerity, drawl, "Well, darlin' what can our boys do to make your job easier?"

The "boys" claimed Cisco's magic bait was hidden in the twinkle of his eye. It always hooked the girls before he reeled them in with flattery and fawning. It didn't matter to Cisco what the women looked like. All women were fair game. He would just as easily ooze over a woman whose genetic composition closely matched a musk ox, as he would over one who could double for Madonna. For Cisco, it was a matter of numbers. If he kept trying, he'd eventually score.

Sometimes even the shop crew were embarrassed by his obsequious drool. The day Cisco reached his peak was the day Belinda from Receiving stopped to check on a parts order. Belinda suffered from a variety of maladies—mainly of the fat and ugly type. Her teeth were a furry grayish green. She strode in five-foot swathes, and equipment would rattle in response to her 310-pound displacement. She was Cisco's ultimate challenge.

As Belinda approached, Cisco was ready for her. Inhaling deeply, he leaned toward Belinda and swooned, "Never smelled such glorious perfume. Just what was it that you splashed on after your morning bath, sugar?"

Belinda was delighted. She cooed and skipped out of the room, sending the machines and equipment off kilter with the percussion of her step. Cisco's eyes followed the sway of her bulging hips as though watching a tennis match. He turned to the crew obscenely rapping, "Booma locka locka locka, booma locka locka locka." Nothing was sacred to Cisco.

Cisco was also known for taking extended breaks and making frequent trips to the vending area. It was not uncommon for him to be gone from his work station for twenty to thirty minutes. The company had contracted with a new vending service earlier that month, and on one of Cisco's trips he saw her for the first time. Cisco was rarely out of control. Very little shocked him, but Wanda was the exception. She had massive muscular arms that exposed a hissing, coiled cobra on her right biceps. Atop her short-sleeved tee-shirt and jeans, she sealed herself with a black leather vest, chaps, and cap. From her back pocket dangled a set of leather thongs. A cigarette dragged from the corner of her mouth, smoldering with an inch long ash clinging precariously to its source. She kneeled down as she pawed through the candy boxes.

Cisco was frozen, speechless, and awestruck. Wanda, oblivious to his presence, swung around with a utility knife in hand to slash one of her unopened candy boxes, barely grazing Cisco's privates.

Cisco shrieked in horror, grabbed his crotch, and collapsed on a nearby chair.

"What the hell are you doin'?" Wanda scolded. "Are you trying to lose your balls, or are you just tired of being a guy?"

Ashen, Cisco looked around to see if any crew members had witnessed this event. "Shit," he muttered to himself, "thank God the guys aren't here."

Attempting to appear composed, Cisco stuttered, "Uh . . . um . . . I was . . . uh . . . just looking to see what new stuff you were adding to the machine. I'll come back later after you're done."

"Whatever turns you on, bud," she grinned fiendishly, waving him off with the utility knife still in hand.

Devastated, Cisco returned to his work station. The crew noticed something was amiss. Cisco's cocky energy usually elbowed its way around the room, egging on the crew to operate at full-tilt. The shroud of quiet set an eerie tone for the rest of the day.

The following morning Cisco was psyched. He'd have enough charm to take on Wanda *and* her cobra. He watched the clock until it was 9:45. Nearly unable to contain himself, he sped off for the vending area in search of Wanda. He knew the vending company kept a desk in the storeroom behind the vending area—she would be there. He peeked around the corner and noticed smoke drifting from a crack in the door. Puffing up his chest, he knocked lightly. The pressure swung the door open, so he was in full view. He beamed with his usual smile and was just about to unleash the charm routine he had been rehearsing all night when Wanda broke in.

"So, asshole, did you come back to apologize for being such a jerk yesterday?" She got up from behind her desk and started to move toward him.

Cisco was so flustered that he stepped backward. He kept eyeing the hissing cobra and gulped at the bulge of her biceps when she placed her hand on her hip.

"You know, there's something about you I like. Did you check your nuts last night to see if you still had them?" Wanda teased.

Cisco glared at her.

"When you did, did you think about me?" she taunted further.

Cisco started to perspire. She was closing in on him. "Who is this Amazon bitch anyway," his mind raced, "and why is she exciting the hell out of me?"

Wanda suddenly reached in her back pocket, grabbed his right wrist, and flipped him around so fast that his head was spinning. Next thing he knew, she was wrapping her leather thongs firmly around his wrists.

"Now what are you going to do?" she dared as her mouth covered his, and her hand moved to unfasten his belt.

Cisco gulped. "Whatever you want," he conceded in disbelief and allowed himself to enjoy.

Shortly after Cisco had left his station, a machine went down. Since Cisco was the lead mechanic, he was always called upon to fix the equipment. One of the crew went to look for him and wandered into the vending area. He noticed that the flimsy decorative frame that surrounded the vending machines was shaking violently. Puzzled, he couldn't imagine what was causing such convulsive vibrations. His investigation led him around the corner to the vending storeroom. There was Cisco, bound and writhing, coupled with Wanda thrusting passionately against the vending area frame.

"Cisco," he interrupted, "the machine went down right after your pants. Get your butt back on the floor. You're disgusting."

"Back off buddy, he'll go when he's delivered," Wanda yelled. "Get the hell outta here."

"Listen, lady, Cisco is on company time, and we have deadlines. Untie him right now, or I'm coming in there."

"Come on," she mocked, "I can take you on too, bozo."

Cisco, immobilized and naked from the waist down, sent a pleading look to his buddy. "Go, will you?" he begged.

The crew member stalked off and reported the incident to Personnel. Cisco received progressive counseling and was told to refrain from sexual activities on company property. The company had the vending contractor transfer Wanda to another location.

Panel Comments Obviously, sexual harassment takes on many faces. Even though we may cheer to see the scales of justice even out a bit, no one—not even such an unsavory character as Cisco—should be in this position. This whole situation probably could have been avoided if Cisco's boss had put a halt to the sexually harassing banter among his co-workers. These actions were not trite or funny and should have been taken quite seriously by the company. We would hope that Cisco's flagrant behavior with Wanda caused the company to provide more limitations on his behavior than simply telling him to take his ardor elsewhere.

While this story presents sexual harassment in the workplace in a new light, it does highlight **Legal Comments** the truism that men, too, can be victims of unlawful sexual harassment. Moreover, even though Wanda was employed by an outside contractor, Cisco's employer could be liable for sexual harassment. As a rule of thumb, an employer may be liable for the unlawful sexual harassment committed by nonemployees if the employee knew or should have known of the misconduct and failed to take prompt, appropriate, corrective action.

Of course, for sexual conduct to be unlawful harassment, it must be unwelcome. It may be difficult for Cisco to establish that Wanda's sexual attentions were "unwelcome."

Finally, aside from whatever liability may arise from possible sexual harassment claims, Wanda would have individual liability for battery and, perhaps, false imprisonment. And *her* employer could be held legally responsible for Wanda's conduct.

LIFE THREATENING LOVES

Rex Cannon came to work extra early that morning prepared to catch up on his swelling paperwork. As personnel manager for 1,400 employees, the work was never ending. Sally, his secretary, was out ill the day before, so yesterday afternoon's mail lay unopened, begging like orphans for attention. He stood at her desk and shuffled through his letters. A CERTIFIED sticker jumped out.

"Uh, oh," he sighed, "this is never a good sign."

The letter was handwritten. He walked to his desk and pulled out a shiny brass letter opener, attacking the envelope viciously. Somehow, he instinctively knew this one would bite.

April 12, 1991

Dear Mr. Cannon:

I am outraged and shocked by your company's practices. I raised my daughter to be a God fearing, respectable young woman. I insisted that she get a good education so that she could support herself in an honorable fashion. Your company is destroying all the values my husband and I instilled in our daughter.

We didn't pay $1,000 for secretarial school tuition so that she could come home and tell me she had to sleep with her boss in order to get her raises. Our daughter graduated at the top of her class. She could get a job anywhere in this city, but she chose your company because you people recruited her right from the technical college. You promised her financial opportunity and career expansion. I don't think the kind of career you're offering her is what she had in mind.

I demand some action. I want Mr. Andrew Marchfield punished for his behavior. If you don't resolve this matter immediately, I will have my attorney file suit, and the newspaper will be breathing down your neck before the month is out.

Yours truly,

(Mrs.) Virginia Hathaway

Rex leaned back in his chair and stared out the window at the frosty cold rain slithering down the glass. "Damn you, Marchfield, it was supposed to be a good day."

Rex checked his watch. It was 8:00 A.M. Sally should be in. He buzzed her on the telephone intercom and asked her to come to his office. Always efficient, Sally arrived with pen and pad poised. "Sally, see if you can get Drew Marchfield to meet me in the cafeteria for a cup of coffee by 8:30. Tell him it's an urgent matter."

Handing her the Hathaway letter, he added, "Please make a copy of this letter, but cover up Mrs. Hathaway's signature line. I don't want it to show up on the copy."

Sally bustled off, and Rex sighed audibly as his mind skipped and jumped through the years. Rex had known Drew for ten years. They went to the same church, took their kids camping together, and served as coaches on little league. Drew Marchfield was a devoted husband and father. Rex had always envied Drew's athletic ability and high energy. He was always the first to pitch in, and he never let you down. His eager smile engendered warmth and assured your trust.

Sally's return to Rex's office interrupted his reverie. She passed both copies of the letter back to Rex and informed him that Drew was en route. Rex grabbed the photocopy and headed for the cafeteria. Just as Rex was lifting his cup, Drew galloped through the doorway. He spotted Rex and put forth his large, fleshy hand and grasped Rex's tightly. "What's up, buddy?"

"I've got a problem, Drew," Rex began cautiously. "Thought maybe you could help me out."

He handed Drew the folded letter and said, "I'd like you to read this letter and help me figure out how I'm going to answer it. Take a few days to think about it, and get back to me on Wednesday. I've got to run—I'm already late for my 8:30."

Rex didn't look back. He left Drew slumped over the letter and took off for his 8:30 meeting. When Rex returned to his office at 10:00, Sally stopped him, put her fingers to her lips, and rolled her eyes.

"What?" Rex asked, not in the mood for her teasing.

All she could do was hold up two fingers, shake her head, and giggle. Rex threw up his hands. "What now?" he thought.

When he walked in his office, there were two blotchy-faced young women, both with noses in tissues and howling as the tears dripped black streaks down their faces. One was Janet Hathaway; the other was Harriet Elmer.

"What's Harriet doing in here, and what's her problem?" wondered Rex.

Just as he was about to ask, the phone rang. It was the Medical Department. Mona Forrest and Lauren Dunn had asked to be excused to go home, the nurse reported. They had arrived within fifteen minutes of each other. Both were crying and extremely distraught.

Rex began to realize that this was more than a coincidence. "Send them to my office," he directed the nurse. "I want to interview them first."

Just as he placed the phone on the receiver, it rang again. This time it was an accounting supervisor. "Rex, something strange is going on. Mary got a phone call and suddenly started crying. She can't stop. I don't know what to do with her."

"Bring her down here," said Rex. "I think I have a hunch."

Rex picked up the phone once again. "Sally, we're likely to get a few more visitors who may be upset. Please send them in. Also, cancel my meetings this morning. I think I'm going to be tied up."

With all five women in his office, Rex began. "Do you girls know each other personally? I mean, are any of you personal friends?" In unison, they all shook their heads, "No."

"Do any of you work in the same department?" Again, a unified "no."

"Did any of you ever work for Drew Marchfield during your tenure with the company?"

They all nodded affirmatively this time. Rex's hunch was confirmed.

He scanned their five red noses. He chose Harriet. She seemed to be the most composed. "Okay, Harriet, let's start with you. Why are you here, and why were you crying?"

Harriet looked at the other four women. "I'd rather not say, it's too personal."

"Fine, then who is willing to tell me why they are here?"

"I will," Mona choked. "That bastard . . . he said . . ."

"What bastard?" Rex interrupted.

"Drew Marchfield," Mona explained.

Rex eyed the four other red noses. They were all steadily focused on Mona.

"Yes, go on," Rex encouraged.

"Drew Marchfield and I had a relationship about two years ago. All of a sudden he called me up out of the blue and said, 'Okay, you big-mouthed bitch; you just cost me my job. Just because you shacked up with me doesn't mean you have to talk to everybody about it.'"

As Mona sobbed and coughed through her story, Rex observed a transformation of the four other red noses. First the tears stopped. Next their eyes widened in horror and turned into narrow, glaring slits of fire.

"He said the exact same thing to me," Mary blurted.

"Me, too, that shit!" yelled Harriet.

"The liar, the lousy liar," howled Janet.

Before the morning was over, four more women joined the group in Rex's office. Each of the nine received the same verbal abuse, and all had been willing lovers of who Rex learned was the "dashing Drew Marchfield." Janet's sexual harassment story, which prompted her mother's letter, was fabricated to ease her pain of Drew's recent rejection. Each woman thought she had been Drew's only transgression. Drew had assured each that they were the "only one."

With nine women scorned—all of whom were now fully informed—Rex knew Drew was a dead man. Rex sequestered the women to conduct further investigation and hastily met with the vice president of the office. After he explained the circumstances, both agreed that Drew needed a quick escape. They made a conference call to the vice president in their West Coast office who was in need of a systems manager. Transfer papers were generated, and Sally made plane reservations. Then she scurried upstairs to gather Drew's belongings. Rex escorted Drew out of the building, briefing him on the way out.

"You are the dumbest son-of-a-bitch I've ever met. Get the hell out of here before these women catch you and skin you alive. The West Coast VP has agreed to take you as his systems manager replacement. You're damn lucky that you're good at what you do and that there was an opening in your area. I don't care what you tell your wife. I'm not gonna tell her anything. But I promise you one thing—if I find out you're making it with our female employees in the future, I'll burn your ass instead of saving it."

Retaining Drew could be an expensive **Panel Comments** decision. It's hard for a leopard to change his spots, and Drew's behavior represents a dangerous pattern that smacks of sexual harassment even if the women were willing lovers. The letter from the young woman's mother did not describe the situation accurately, but that does not condone Drew's behavior. Ethically, an individual in a position of power over other employees, who consistently uses his position to set up sexual liaisons, does not deserve to be protected and retained. The company's response sounds too much like an "old boys" reaction—the "you shouldn't have gotten so greedy or been caught" response. The company's actions send a poor message to female employees concerning the company's opinion of them. We also think that if anyone would leak this to the press, the company would have a public relations nightmare.

All too often, sexual harassment situations evolve from originally consensual relationships **Legal Comments** that turn sour. Thereafter, when one party tries to continue the relationship, the previously acceptable conduct becomes unwelcome and sometimes crosses the line into illegality. For this reason, employers are well-advised to recommend that employees refrain from sexual affairs with subordinates or even co-workers.

In this situation, it is questionable whether any unlawful sexual harassment took place. The women were "willing lovers" of Marchfield and evidently no pressure was brought to bear on them in return for their sexual favors (e.g., "sleep with me for the promotion"). An affair between a manager and subordinate may not be smart, but it is not automatically unlawful.

Given Marchfield's propensities, I would seriously question the wisdom of simply transferring him. He appears to be courting a sexual harassment lawsuit. Retaining him would substantially increase the company's risk of expensive and time-consuming litigation.

THE CASE OF THE MISSING PIANO COVER

Frank felt something was amiss. He abruptly stopped sweeping and leaned against his push broom, peering through the proscenium. Standing slightly left of center stage, he breathed deeply and inhaled the familiar scent of the freshly-laid wood flooring. The corporation carpenters and electricians had put the finishing touches on its newly-remodeled auditorium only last week. Frank beamed as he nodded at the state-of-the-art speakers and lights. "Best acoustics and light show in the city," he proudly commented aloud.

As Frank panned the plush velvet seats, he envisioned the room flowing with people. He was grateful to work for a company that cared so much for its employees. He shifted his eyes back and forth, back and forth. Pivoting slightly to the right, he saw it. There it was—the grand piano—slick and shimmering even with the lights low.

"God it's a beauty," Frank thought, filling up further with pride. Then it struck him. Where was the cover—the thick, brown quilted cover—to protect the piano from dust? He had special-ordered it from the manufacturer and had received it only three days ago.

Frank flushed. He was a man of order. He was responsible for protecting "his" auditorium. First he checked the wings, next the empty boxes back stage, and finally examined each row of the audience seats, like a farmer checking his crop. The cover had vanished. Puzzled, Frank returned to his office.

After several hours Fumiko and Sun, two trustworthy workers on his cleaning crew, gently knocked on Frank's office door. Weighted down by the bulky brown quilting, the two fragile women presented their offering. "We find in basement," Fumiko explained.

Frank puffed up his checks and squinted his eyes, "Where in the basement?"

"In changing room. Can put down, please? Is heavy," Fumiko said.

Frank was relieved. He was not looking forward to completing the paperwork required for stolen property and having to submit a purchase order for a new cover. His budget was already overextended. He got up from his desk and nodded as the women unloaded the cover in his outstretched arms. He thanked them, walked to the auditorium, and lovingly replaced the cover on the piano.

The next evening when Frank cruised through the auditorium on his nightly check, his first concern was the piano cover. Expecting to be comforted by its cocoa quilting, Frank's eyes bulged in disbelief. Gone again! Heart racing, he headed straight for the basement and switched the light on in the changing room. The large room was empty except for five make-up tables against the outside wall. Then he looked at the opposite wall. The entire wall was mirrored. He saw his scowl reflected back as he glanced around the room. Then he spotted the cover. In the far corner, with sides neatly tucked under and its base spread out like a picnic blanket, was the errant piano cover. Grumbling under his breath, Frank grabbed the cover and slammed the door behind him.

Each evening Frank checked for the piano cover. Each evening it was gone, and Frank found it tidily spread in exactly the same corner of the changing room. Frank's initial worry turned first to anger and then to rage. He was certain someone from the day crew was playing a practical joke. He'd fix them. He'd turn it over to security. "Messing with company property will get their goddamn butts fired," he muttered menacingly to himself.

Security set up immediate surveillance, and Frank received the following report:

On Monday, June 10, at 11:45 A.M., our officer stationed in the projection room observed a white male with wavy blond hair, approximately 30 years old and 6'2" tall, enter the rear of the auditorium, march directly down to the front of the stage, hoist himself up, deftly slip off the piano cover, sling it over his shoulder, and disappear in the wings.

Approximately one minute later, a second officer, who was hidden from view, observed a white male with the same description enter the changing room. Within two minutes the officer also observed a white female with brown hair and blue eyes, approximately 5'5" and 25 years old, slip into the same changing room. Security then observed a loud click, suggesting the door was bolted.

Sounds coming from the room were whispered conversation, giggles, and moans. Both suspects remained in the room for approximately 45 minutes. The male left first, followed by the female within one minute. Both officers observed similar behavior for three consecutive days.

A check of employee files and photo identification indicate the male to be Roger Rainwater, employed as a graphic artist. He is single, has excellent attendance, has been with the company for eight years and has received above satisfactory performance ratings during the last three years. The female is Melissa Coleman, secretary to the vice president of facilities planning. She has been employed for four years. She also has excellent attendance and her past two performance ratings were excellent.

On June 17, both employees met with the personnel manager, were confronted with the evidence, and signed a statement admitting their unauthorized use of the piano cover. Both were told to refrain from further lovemaking on company property. Both Mr. Rainwater and Ms. Coleman also agreed to absorb the cost of having the piano cover dry cleaned. The matter was closed on June 18.

Panel Comments We're surprised the employees involved in removing the piano cover didn't grow suspicious themselves when the cover they left on the floor kept finding its way back to the piano. We hope they're not in jobs where understanding cause and effect is important!

Legal Comments Before conducting any surveillance of employees, it is prudent to obtain the advice of counsel. Such surveillance may give rise to invasion of privacy claims. While employers generally have discretion to monitor their own work place, there are limits that vary from state to state.

2
SYSTEMS BEATERS

City, state, and federal government employees operate under an oppressive burden of rules, regulations, policies, and procedures. Any attempt at creative freedom is virtually stifled by the bureaucratic morass in which they struggle. This environment makes civil servants excellent candidates for beating the system. To trip the big machine over its own rules and regulations offers a great deal of personal satisfaction along with some monetary reward. We probably could feel more compassionate for this group if it weren't for the fact that it's our tax dollars that pay for their shenanigans.

PROMOTIONAL ADIPOSE

Loren knew he had a problem the moment young Tessie Raghey waddled her 292-pound hulk, with arms flapping like lifeless sausages from her short-sleeved print tunic, into his office. Tessie's stubby right hand held a large brown envelope; her left, an oversized canvas purse.

"Please sit down, Ms. Raghey. I'm Loren Froelich, the human resources manager. How can I help you?"

Loren watched Tessie slowly move sideways and then back herself carefully into the chair across from his desk. Her breath was unusually labored for such a young woman, and her enormous chest heaved with such motion that Loren started to get dizzy. He sat down quickly to steady himself.

Once Tessie managed to get comfortable, she issued a short grunt and then smugly demanded, "My doctor says I'm too fat to file. You gotta get me a sit-down job."

"Well, just what is it that you can't do, Ms. Raghey?" Loren asked.

"I can't be bendin' on my knees, the doctor says, and the aisles are gettin' too narrow for me to squeeze through," she said handing him the doctor's report. Then she removed a white bag from her large purse and pulled out a plump doughnut.

Loren shook his head and smiled. Tessie had him. The only other jobs in Salary Grade 1 in their regional office were housekeeper and groundskeeper, both requiring the employee to stand or bend. Despite the fact that Tessie's performance was only marginal on her current job, he would have to promote her to a higher level job. The policy required that the government find her another job within the system in order to accommodate her medical condition. If there were no appropriate jobs in the current grade, then they had to use the next higher salary grade.

Since she had been on the job only four months, she was at the minimum of her salary range. So, she would not only get promoted but also receive a raise to bring her to the new salary grade minimum.

Tessie was pleased with herself. Although she was only eighteen years old and this was her first real job, she figured out how to milk the system in less than five months. She just sat there devouring her jelly doughnut and brushing off the powdered sugar that fell on her lap, while Loren scanned his list of available jobs in Salary Grade 2. She'd work the Grade 2 job until she could find another free ride to hitch from the system. It gave Tessie great pleasure to know that she could look forward to a career of discovering all the ways to manipulate the bureaucracy to her advantage.

Panel Comments Tessie is clearly using her weight as a convenient goldbricking technique. We recommend that the human resources manager make a literal interpretation of the doctor's report. The report said that Tessie can't bend at the knees, not that she needs a "sit-down" job. The "can't squeeze through the aisle" excuse sounds like her conclusion, not the doctor's. We would modify a less desirable Salary Grade 1 job for her until she legitimately earns a promotion. Perhaps she could function as a housekeeper, with no more than bend-at-the-waist responsibilities.

Legal Comments As the familiar joke goes, one of the reasons that the Soviet Union is in trouble is because everybody there is a public employee. The bureaucracy, regulatory control, and formalism surrounding public employment are difficult to describe to someone who has not personally dealt with the situation.

This story illustrates my point. Tessie may be a handicapped person (obese) under state law and perhaps under the Americans with Disabilities Act of 1990. Under these laws, employers must not discriminate on the basis of handicap against an individual who is otherwise qualified for the position. If the person's handicap interferes with his or her ability to perform the job, the employer must try to reasonably accommodate that handicap but does not have to incur an undue hardship. Here, if Tessie is not able to perform the job for which she was hired and if no reasonable accommodation can solve the problem, the company is not required to continue her in its employ.

That is the legal obligation. Any employer may impose upon itself greater obligations than that required by the law, and many public employers have done so. Thus, in this situation, the public employer's "policy" goes beyond its legal obligation and apparently requires this employee to be promoted. Given this bizarre result, a rethinking of the policy may be desirable.

THE GLITCH THAT LOST KRISTA

Chas was quite pleased. He was instrumental in redesigning the organization and implementing the communication program. He arranged for small-group meetings so that employees could understand the need for reorganization. The process took him nearly a month of continuous meetings, but the response was favorable. The employees cooperated and helped make the transition very smooth. After six weeks, the first productivity report showed a fifteen percent decrease in expenses, and morale seemed stable. The agency had plans to administer a work-climate study after twelve months. Chas was immersed in the glowing productivity report when his assistant, Suzanne, walked in his office.

"Here they are, fresh off the presses, our first run since the reorganization," Suzanne chirped.

Chas looked up from his desk puzzled, "What?"

"The performance review reminders," Suzanne responded. "You know, every month we get a printout for those employees due for their annual performance review. They have little computer-generated postcards that we send out to the managers."

"Oh, right, right. Go ahead and send them out," Chas said, still preoccupied with his productivity report.

Several days later he got a call from Gordon Fishman, the information officer.

"Say, Chas," Gordon began, "I just got the computer reminder to give Krista Reed, one of my former clerks, her performance review. Since we reorganized, Krista doesn't work for me any more."

Krista was fairly far down in the organization, so her name would not show up on the major charts. Chas remembered hiring her about three years ago for a simple, routine clerk job. She was rather plain, not very bright, but quite pleasant. When her performance reviews had crossed his desk, there was nothing unusual. They were mostly peppered with satisfactories. She had received only one promotion in three years and tended to blend right into the agency.

"Well, what happened to her?" Chas asked.

"I'm not really sure, but I think she's reporting to Bill Acton in Administration. Try him," Gordon responded.

Chas looked up Bill's extension. "Say, Bill, this is Chas Vidmar. We have a performance appraisal due on Krista Reed, and I understand she reports to you now."

"Krista Reed? Nope, not me. I think she was shipped over to Tracy Karras after the reorganization. Give Tracy a call," Bill suggested.

Chas tapped out Tracy's four-digit extension. "Ms. Karras's office, Jane speaking."

"Hi, Jane, this is Chas Vidmar. Is Tracy available?"

"Sorry, Mr. Vidmar, but Tracy is out of the office at a meeting with one of our vendors."

"Oh," he paused, "well, maybe you can help me. Does Krista Reed report to your section?"

"That name doesn't sound familiar, but I'll check. Can you hold?"

"Sure."

Chas waited while he scanned his own personnel computer runs. There was Krista Reed's name all right. She still retained Gordon Fishman's budget code, but the section reassignment code was blank. That's why the performance appraisal reminder defaulted to Gordon. "Where the hell could she be?" he thought.

Jane returned to the line. "Sorry, Mr. Vidmar, but we don't have her here."

"Thanks, Jane." Chas rang off and sat at his desk bewildered. The agency had over two thousand people and he wasn't about to send out a missing-rewards memo on Krista. She was getting her paycheck. That must be a clue.

"Rats," he thought, after he checked with payroll. "My luck, she has her pay direct-deposited, with the confirmation mailed to her home. "Her home," he thought, "maybe she's at home. I'll try there." For an entire week Chas periodically called Krista's number—no answer or busy. He was getting very frustrated.

Chas usually worked through his lunch, grabbing some junk food from the vending machine. Today he felt especially hungry for some reason, so he ventured into the employee cafeteria. He filled his tray from the deli bar and passed through the register.

Seated a few tables from the register was Krista Reed! Chas couldn't believe his eyes. His surprise almost caused him to set his *Coke* off balance. He regained control and casually sauntered over to Krista, who was seated with some other women. There was an available seat across from her.

"Mind if I join you?" Chas asked politely.

"Sure, no problem," Krista smiled.

"So, Krista, it's been a long time since we've talked. How have you been?"

"Pretty good."

"So where are you working now that we've reorganized?" he asked.

"I'm glad you asked," she responded sincerely. "When everyone got their printout of where to be reassigned, the section for me was blank. My boss was tied up in meetings that day, so I didn't get to discuss it with him. Even though the move wasn't scheduled for two weeks, I wasn't able to get to him because I left that Friday for my two-week vacation. So, when I returned, everyone was in their new offices, and my boss, as you know, was shipped over to Building G across the complex. My section was split three ways, so I didn't even know which group to follow and haven't known what to do. I've felt really lost and kind of upset that the agency has forgotten about me. So I just came to work and visited with friends in the various break rooms, and then I'd sit through all three lunch sessions. That part has been a lot of fun, but to tell the truth, I've been getting kinda bored."

"That's terrible, Krista," Chas feigned sympathetically.

"And not only that," she added "with all these lunches I've eaten over the past several weeks, I've gained nearly eight pounds!"

Chas was astounded. He knew Krista wasn't a rocket scientist, but how could she spend over a month occupying her day having one long lunch, just hoping someone might notice? Incredibly, no one did notice, and Krista appeared deadly serious and wholly sincere. Rather than embarrass himself and the whole agency for the major snafu, Chas politely suggested to Krista that she return with him to his office. He reviewed the organizational design study and determined where Krista should logically be located. Chas contacted the section manager and notified him that he was sending Krista on up. Then he put a change action through to the computer to ensure that the elusive Krista would once again have a home.

Many employees are overlooked and treated as
Panel Comments if they don't exist. With little attention and feedback, they become bored and complacent. This management problem may have encouraged Krista to "play dumb and stay lost." Any time a company undergoes a reorganization, it should include a *personal* meeting with *every* employee to explain or discuss the impact on the employee's job. Despite the fact that the agency did not handle the reorganization appropriately, it has the right to hold Krista responsible for her actions. She should have received discipline for being AWOL.

Legal Comments This story demonstrates an often overlooked point. Employees have no obligation to seek out work. Whether private or public, it is management's obligation and legal right to insist that employees perform assigned duties in a satisfactory manner. This seems obvious, but many employers are reluctant to exercise their basic right to tell employees to go back to work when such situations arise.

STICKING TO HER KNITTING

Sheila was the human resources representative assigned to the Accounting Department and had been working with the unit head for well over four months. The agency had planned to automate the entire unit, which would cause the elimination of thirteen jobs. The computer had been installed, and the unit was operating on dual systems during the testing period. The agency expected to be weaned from manual systems by month's end.

Sheila had considered the two available alternatives for dealing with the surplus employees. One option was to place the surplus employees into different jobs. The agency's human resources guidelines stated that these people must be placed in jobs that required similar skills and pay equivalent to that of the position they were leaving. Thus, employees would continue to report to work and receive full pay until they accepted a job that met the skill and pay criteria. The flaw in this policy was that the employee had to find the proposed position "acceptable." If the employee cited a legitimate reason why he or she couldn't accept the position, Sheila would have to continue her search, and the employee would remain on full pay during this nonproductive time.

The second option was to declare a reduction in force. This was rarely the preferred choice because it activated the bumping policy, which entitled a displaced employee with more seniority to bump a less senior employee from a job in the same job family. The bumping process tended to trigger a chain reaction. With thirteen employees involved, it was very likely that numerous other employees would be pushed into different jobs. This would have a disruptive effect on everyone, with many employees having no idea how to perform the job in which they eventually landed.

To compound matters, there was always the problem of appeals. In cases like this, there is a great opportunity for error, and invariably someone will claim they were unfairly bumped. If the "bumpee" wins the case, Sheila would have to re-bump everyone down the line and disrupt everyone all over again. The whole thing was a thankless, negative nightmare of time and paper work. Given that the displaced staff contained highly senior people, Sheila felt that a reduction in force and its attendant bumping would have limited positive outcomes. From her standpoint, a reduction in force would ultimately reduce productivity and decrease morale.

In her crusade to avoid the bumping beast, Sheila concentrated her efforts for nearly a month on identifying jobs for the thirteen employees. She combed all other units throughout the agency. She checked for upcoming retirements and planned expansions in her attempt to find potential openings and suitable assignments for the baker's dozen. Sheila worked very hard toward achieving her goal. She communicated the situation throughout the agency and put a freeze on any new hires. All units had to consider the people from the displaced group first. Sheila's strategy paid off. There were only five people left who would be idle when the unit officially threw the switch.

The remaining five were assigned to an unoccupied office on the fourth floor. The office had no furniture except for a few chairs and large table. To kill the boredom, Sheila arranged for the Training Department to loan the group its television. The group was glued to it most of the time, except when Training borrowed it back for special sessions.

Over the course of three months, Sheila steadfastly attempted to get the employees placed. One by one, appropriate assignments came up and each moved out. The only person remaining was a middle-aged fuss-budget named Edna Blake. Sheila had proposed four jobs to Edna, and Edna refused each. She always found something unacceptable about each job. Edna's last excuse was that the job required bending, and she suffered from vertigo.

Edna had been the lone holdout of the group and remained in the room, reporting diligently every day at 8:30 A.M. and leaving not a moment before 5:00 P.M. One day, out of frustration, Sheila stopped by to ask Edna how she could stand spending the whole day in an empty room. Edna remarked that she was quite content to wait until the agency found her the right job. She enjoyed knitting or crocheting while she watched television. She said that she liked the idea of being in the know with the outside world. Edna told Sheila that she had set up a wonderful routine. Her day began with the last segment of the *Today* show; then she moved on to the talk shows, sandwiched in some soaps, and ended the afternoon with reruns of *Gilligan's Island.* Of course, she took her regular coffee and lunch breaks so that she wouldn't lose touch with the other employees. She didn't want to miss out on any important agency matters.

Edna was a master at the game. She knew that few jobs were perfect fits, and those jobs had no immediate openings in sight. She also knew that Human Resources did not want to bump anyone from the perfect fits because they were held by senior people, and those folks would have the right to bump less senior employees. So, one bump—just one bump—would have a disastrous domino effect.

After five fruitless months with Edna continuing to turn down jobs, Sheila had an opportunity to leave the agency and take a job in the private sector. To this day, she doesn't know how long it took to place Edna. The last thing that Sheila remembers was Edna proudly showing her the three sweaters and eleven afghans she had racked up as Christmas presents and mumbling something about trying her hand at hooking a rug.

Panel Comments This woman may not be bothered by her lack of work because the organization made the situation too comfortable. A more realistic approach would have been to take away the television and knitting and put her on some temporary duty that would make her long for a nicer, more permanent arrangement.

Legal Comments Removing the television set would be within the employer's rights here and could have positive impact on Edna's willingness to accept other employment. Sometimes a little self-help is the easiest solution to employment-related problems.

3

ODD DUCKS AND NONCONFORMISTS

Every company has a cadre of colorful characters. You can find them anywhere from the mail room to the boardroom. These employees seem to have an unending capacity to cajole, irritate, astonish, or frustrate. Typically, they are outstanding performers, so we tolerate their eccentricities and tend to keep them on staff. One thing is certain—they leave a lasting impression. It's not surprising, then, that in our reverie, we often find ourselves repeating sighs of disbelief and continue to shake our heads in amazement as we are reminded of their unconventional antics.

HORSING AROUND

Joe discovered it late Saturday afternoon after Marcie had already left. He decided to wait until Monday to confront her about it. He looked at the unpacked boxes in his sparkling new office to try to calm down. He couldn't. He was still broiling when Marcie breezed through the door and casually plopped down on the chair across from his desk. She was grinning her famous carefree grin.

"Hi, Joe, so what's up?"

"What's up?" he mocked her, attempting to control his anger. "I'd like an explanation about last Saturday's display in the lobby. I can't believe that you would . . ."

"I don't know what the big deal is all about," she interrupted. "Personally, I thought I was doing the company a favor by coming in on Saturday to help with the move to our new facility. Giving up my Saturday was a major sacrifice. It interfered with the time I always spend with Hattie. Overtime pay or not, Hattie expects to see me on Saturdays, and I just couldn't skip. She'd be too disappointed. And since she's boarded only three miles from the office, I thought, 'Why not?' So I rode her over, parked her in the lobby, and pitched in to do my share. After all, it was only for a few hours."

Joe was not buying it.

"Quit looking at me like that, Joe. Really, I just think you're making a mountain out of a molehill. Look, we were vacating the building, and horses just do those things. It's perfectly natural. Besides, a cleaning crew was already scheduled to follow for the final sweep to disinfect and deodorize."

Joe was still not talking. He just sat there and glared at her.

"Look, Joe, we got our deposit back," she said scrambling. "No one was hurt, and we're all moved. I don't understand why you're so upset."

Joe let his shock over Marcie's outrageous behavior cloud his ability to properly handle this case. He should have told Marcie that by leaving a large animal unattended in a public building, she endangered her co-workers and put the company at unnecessary risk. If the horse became frightened, people could have been hurt and more than a cleaning crew would be required to handle the property damage. This approach would have given Marcie a realistic perspective on her actions.

To paraphrase General Schwartzkopf, this episode of equine scatology does not appear to pose any particular legal issue.

A STICKY SITUATION

Hilda was permanently attached to the processing unit. She'd been there for twelve years and hoped to stay the next ten until she retired. Hilda was from a small farm community and had moved to Des Moines to go to vocational school. She loved her job and had no interest in promotions. Her perfect attendance certificates, suspended by colorful fruit magnets, sang from the side of her desk. She had received a certificate for every year except one. In her eighth year, she missed a day for an emergency root canal. Joyce, her supervisor, often remarked that she had never seen such a dedicated employee. Hilda preferred to work through coffee breaks and left the area no more than twice a day to use the restroom. Because of her top performance and tenure, most everyone overlooked Hilda's peculiarities.

New employees were usually appalled by Hilda's appearance when first meeting her. Hilda's anklets and loafers, coupled with her frumpy sleeveless cotton house dresses and unshaven arms and legs, raised a few eyebrows. Her oversized white cardigan sweater, pilled with wear, draped the back of her chair for nearly nine years. It almost seemed a part of the furniture. She reserved her sweater for days when the temperature dropped. The new clerks would muffle their giggles as Hilda would throw the sweater over her shoulders and secure it with two little alligator clips connected with a makeshift chain of safety pins.

That was just Hilda. She was basically a loner and didn't bother anyone. She'd greet everyone in the morning, work steadily all day, and wave good-bye at night. Hilda wasn't much for socializing. She grabbed a soft drink from the vending machine and spent lunch at her desk while everyone else escaped to the cafeteria.

Hilda's desk was an arsenal of supplies. She happily entertained herself during lunch. She kept her cross-stitch, newspapers, and all her sundries in her desk. If someone needed anything—an aspirin, a cough drop—they knew Hilda had a supply.

One day the unit supervisor was surprised by a group of eleven clerks crammed in her office.

Martha stepped forward as the spokesperson. "Joyce, we've got a problem."

Joyce couldn't imagine what could be wrong. She made it a habit of talking with the staff regularly to solicit feedback and concerns. Having all of them in there except Hilda had her totally baffled.

"Well, please, tell me what's bothering you," Joyce responded.

"It's Hilda," Martha replied.

"What about Hilda?"

"It's . . . it's embarrassing, Joyce."

"Tell her," Susie urged Martha.

Joyce sat patiently eyeing the group. They were fidgeting and looking very strange.

"Well it all started when we found this gooey, yucky stuff on the file drawer handles," Martha began.

"Gooey, yucky stuff? Like what?" Joyce asked.

"Well, it was this glob of stuff. It wasn't sticky like honey or greasy like vaseline exactly; it was just clear. Then it dried and flaked off."

"Like children's glue?"

"Not exactly."

"Well, do you have a sample?"

"Not with me. I didn't want to touch the stuff," she said, wrinkling her nose and making a sour face.

"Well, where is it?"

"We'll show you, but first we want to tell you something."

Joyce's curiosity was piqued. Just what were they driving at? "So tell me. I'm waiting."

"We think Hilda is using some kind of ointment and not washing her hands after using it. Then she goes to the files and leaves her globs. We also found some on the vending machine."

"What makes you think it's Hilda?"

"Well, we've all been watching her very carefully lately. Four of us have seen the same thing. It all starts when she gets this weird, tense look on her face—almost like a grimace. When that happens, she immediately goes in her right-hand top drawer. Then she pulls out this tube of stuff and squeezes this clear glob onto two or three of her fingers of her right hand. Then she sticks both hands under her desk, squirms around in her chair, and gets an intense look on her face. In a few moments, the tension drains from her face, she smiles, caps the tube, and puts it back in the drawer. Sometimes she stays at her desk. Other times she dashes off to the files. This happens three or four times a day."

"So, you really aren't sure what she's doing then?"

"Well, we think we are."

"What do you mean?"

"Well—and I'm sorry, Joyce—but we had to . . ."

"Had to what?"

"One of us stayed late last night and opened up her drawer to find out what the stuff was."

Joyce was dying to know, but she had to act upset. "You went in her desk!?"

"Well, we suspected, but we just had to know for sure. Look, Joyce, she's using *Vagisil*—you know that anti-itch ointment—and she's not washing her hands after! God, it's so gross!"

All the others squealed their "yeichs," "auughs," and "blechs" in unison.

"That's enough. I appreciate your informing me, and I'll take care of it. Don't do any more filing until I get the janitorial crew to disinfect the cabinets. Work on your processing jobs instead. Say nothing to Hilda."

Before Joyce could do anything, she needed to verify the facts. The tough part was doing so without obviously intruding on Hilda's privacy. Joyce walked over to Hilda's desk.

"Good morning, Hilda."

"Hi, Joyce."

"Say, Hilda, I seem to be out of aspirin. Would you happen to have one?"

"Sure," Hilda responded, opening her right-hand desk drawer, revealing the *Vagisil* nestled next to the cough drops.

Hilda fingered through the drawer and located the bottle. When she started to open it to pull out a couple of aspirin, Joyce pointed to the tube in the drawer and asked, "Gee, what's that, Hilda?"

"It's . . . uhm . . . sorta like a cream," Hilda answered as her face reddened slightly.

"Oh, you mean for dry skin?"

"Not exactly," Hilda hesitated, "it's for itching. I've been itching something terrible the past week."

"Could you excuse me, Hilda, I just remembered something?"

"Don't you want your aspirin?"

"Oh, yes, thank you."

Joyce ran to her office, pitched the aspirin like they contained demons, and dashed for the restroom to wash her hands. Then she called human resources for help on how to handle the situation. They advised her to explain the health hazards to Hilda and send her to Medical for counseling by the nurse.

So, before sending her down to the nurse, Joyce asked Hilda to come to her office. "Hilda, have you been applying your *Vagisil* at your work station?"

"Yes, Joyce, but I'm careful. No one can see what I'm doing. I just hate to miss any time from my job. The ladies' room is all the way down the hall. It seems so far to go. I don't want to miss time."

"Poor Hilda," Joyce thought, "always the dedicated employee." Then she said aloud, "Hilda I'm going to send you to the nurse. She may be able to refer you to a doctor who can help you with your problem. In the meantime I don't want you to apply the ointment at your desk. And you must wash your hands afterward. What you're doing is presenting a health hazard to the other employees. Do you understand?"

"What if I get some paper towels to keep in my drawer."

"No, Hilda, that's not acceptable," Joyce said firmly.

"I just don't want to lose time," Hilda fretted.

"It will be okay," Joyce tried to assure her.

"How about those *Wash'n Dri* towelettes? I could use those," Martha offered.

"No, Hilda, it's not sanitary. You must go to the restroom each time and wash your hands *with soap and water.* Now, if you'll please speak to the nurse, she may be able to send you to a doctor who can help solve your problem once and for all."

Joyce watched Hilda walked off dejectedly. Poor Hilda, she just hated having to miss . . . .

Panel Comments Personal hygiene is one of the most difficult subjects for a supervisor to handle, because it is so personal. Personnel advised Joyce correctly. The immediate supervisor, not Personnel, should deliver the bad news. This situation is tough enough without further humiliating the employee by sending him or her to Personnel to have a relative stranger deal with this unpleasant task. However, Joyce should call the nurse and advise her of the circumstances before Hilda talks with her. By providing the nurse with some context, she will be in the best position to assist Hilda.

THE GENDER GAP

"Hi, I'm Ruth Eldon, please have a seat." Ruth smiled and motioned to the side chair next to her desk as she looked up at the six-foot-two-inch figure standing before her. "She must be new, I haven't seen her before," Ruth thought as she scanned the woman's massive frame and broad shoulders.

The tall woman sat down and responded, "Thank you, my name is Lois Moorehead. I've just transferred from Sacramento to the division here in San Diego. Since I was married last weekend, I'd like to add a spouse to my benefits coverage."

"Well, congratulations, Lois!" Ruth smiled. "Let me call up your record." She entered "Moorehead" into her computer, and the record flashed before her with Lois's complete work history.

"I see you've been with our Sacremento office for six years. Welcome to San Diego, I'm sure you'll love it here," Ruth added and handed Lois a form.

"Now, Lois, if you'll just give me your husband's name, I'll change your last name and add his as spouse directly to your computer record. You'll just need to sign this benefit change form for our records," Ruth instructed efficiently.

Lois began slowly. "*Her name is Charlotte,* and I won't be changing my last name."

Ruth wasn't sure if she heard Lois correctly. Did this woman just say her spouse was a woman? Ruth's eyes glanced first at Lois, then over to her screen. The record flashed back:

```
MOOREHEAD, LOIS R.        BIRTH DATE: 2-28-60
SEX: F                    MARITAL STATUS: S
```

Ruth struggled to maintain her composure and nervously cleared her throat. "I'm sorry, Lois, but we have you listed here as a female. It's my understanding that . . . um . . . homosexuals cannot be legally married in this state. So we can't cover you for a female spouse."

Lois opened her folder and laid some documents on Ruth's desk and said politely, "If you'll notice, I've provided you with two documents. The first is a marriage license from the State of California. The second is my birth certificate. You'll notice that the sex states 'male.' "

Ruth examined the documents and could hardly believe what she saw. They were valid and stated exactly what Lois had indicated, except they both showed the name *Louis* Moorehead instead of *Lois* Moorehead. Ruth put her hand up to her face, massaging her chin and cheeks in hopes of magically rubbing out a solution. She decided to start with some questions.

"Lois, help me out if you can. I have three basic questions. Why is it you use the name *Lois* instead of your real name *Louis*, why do we have you listed as a female, and why do you dress as a female if you are a male?"

"I had a sex change operation before I came to the company."

"Oh . . . well . . . then you *are* a female," Ruth maintained.

"Physically, yes. Legally, no. I never had my birth certificate changed. So, according to the laws of the State of California, I'm still a male."

"Well, do you intend to continue dressing as a female and using the female restroom facilities?" Ruth asked.

"Of course," Lois responded.

"Well, I don't think that will be acceptable to our insurance carrier. If you want to be considered a male, you'll have to dress like a male and use the male restroom," Ruth asserted.

"Since I no longer have male equipment, consider me neuter."

Ruth chuckled to herself thinking, "We don't have a computer code for neuter." Then she responded. "No, I don't think neuter will be acceptable."

"I think you need to understand something," Lois began. "My wife is very, very ill. She can't work and doesn't have a job. The state will not give her assistance because they have a regulation that if a person is married to a spouse who has insurance coverage, the person must be covered by the spouse's insurance. If we cannot get her the medical treatment she needs, she could die. Because the treatments are so expensive, no one will give her care if she isn't covered by state assistance or my insurance."

Ruth grew more compassionate. "I understand your dilemma, Lois, but your circumstances are rather unusual. Let me work on this and see what I can do."

After Lois left Ruth's office, Ruth immediately called corporate counsel and the director of benefits to help resolve the matter. The benefits director was concerned with the company's moral obligations. Corporate counsel was concerned about potential liability. Specifically, what if the wife dies due to lack of medical care? Will the company be responsible? A final determination had not been made at the time the story was related. Lois is still on the books as a woman, and the spouse is not covered.

Panel Comments More often than not, the best friend of the human resources manager is common sense. When confronted with alleged facts (in this case the legal documents) and reality (this guy is a woman), rely on reality. Or more simply put, if it looks, sounds, and acts like a duck, it's probably a duck. Then call your lawyer.

Legal Comments This story highlights an important matter for human resources professionals. Homosexuals and transsexuals are not protected by the *federal* laws prohibiting employment discrimination. Also, they are not considered handicapped under the Americans with Disabilities Act of 1990. However, at least one *state* (Wisconsin) and several *cities* (e.g., San Francisco and New York) have local laws that prohibit discrimination on the basis of sexual preference. To minimize the risk of inadvertent violations, employers must be familiar with the laws of all jurisdictions where they are engaged in business.

If this story had arisen in a jurisdiction that barred sexual preference discrimination, Lois might be able to claim that she was being treated differently vis-a-vis dependent coverage than nonhomosexuals or nontranssexuals.

DOGGED PERSISTENCE

Jeff headed a small scientific research company. His example set the dress code for the office. He'd arrive in a muscle shirt and jogging shorts or a running suit— whatever his plans demanded. Magnetic, handsome, and fully fit at forty-nine, he had completed his fourth race in the famed Hawaiian Ironman Triathlon.

Three months preceding the event, he began daily training. He moved his touring bike to his office, removed the front wheel, and mounted it on a stationary frame. Then he'd pedal the hours away as he read scientific journals that were perched on the stand mounted to his handle bars. He also had his secretary rig a low-level podium to another piece of exercise equipment he dragged into the office, so he could read while working his arms for the swimming segment.

To prepare for the marathon portion of the event, he ran during his lunch hour, which he extended to two hours. To keep him company, Mik, his Irish Setter, helped maintain the pace. Jeff brought Mik to the office every day during training. Mik relaxed in Jeff's office until it was time for their lunch run. Mik instinctively knew the time and eagerly accompanied Jeff. Jeff looked forward to the event each year. He was going to begin training next month.

The company leased about 10,000 square feet of space in a suburban commercial complex. They shared the building with a bank and an insurance company. Jeff's employees often came in and out at odd hours. They were given free reign to accomplish their jobs and dress as they pleased. They rarely dealt with the public and suited up in business attire only when necessary. A casual dress code and liberal working hours created a special atmosphere. Employees were comfortable, committed, and motivated. They liked having control of their lives, and few abused the policy. Those who did were forced out by their peers. No one tolerated free loaders.

Unfortunately, the neighboring insurance company and banking employees were unhappy. They resented the small company's freedom and casual dress. The landlord received complaints from neighboring companies that Jeff's company was having a negative effect on the morale of their employees. These companies also informed Jeff of their concerns by certified letter. Jeff thought they were stupid and ignored them. His company was building its own facility and would be moving in six months. Jeff couldn't be bothered with their pettiness.

"Let those dumb shits try to evict me," he thought, discarding the letter. "By the time they get their act together, we'll be out of here anyway."

The day had arrived to begin training, so Jeff brought Mik to the office. The bank employees were furious. Three women were especially provoked about Mik. Since complaints to the landlord were ineffective, they conspired to call the health department and fabricate a story. They complained that they had developed an infection from the toilet seat because Mik had nosed his way into the ladies' restroom. When Jeff received a complaint letter from the state health department, he became enraged.

"Those lard-assed bitches," he muttered aloud. "There's no way I'm going to let Mik take the blame."

Jeff immediately dialed up his veterinarian and told him the story. The veterinarian agreed to write the following letter in Mik's defense and sent a copy to the bank's branch manager.

Attention State Health Department:

I am writing in response to the complaint against Jeff Camden's dog, Mik.

There is no way that a canine can transmit a sexual disease to three females via a toilet seat. The only way that three women could contract the same infection at the same time would be if they were all having sex with the same man.

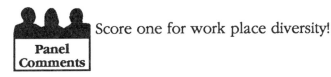 Score one for work place diversity!

Let's hope that Jeff and the veterinarian have paid up libel insurance; they may need it. While there was some legal justification to communicate to the health department about Mik's inability to transmit diseases to women, it is difficult to perceive any justification for the third sentence in the veterinarian's letter or for his decision to send a copy to the bank. Imputing sexual misconduct to a woman is one of those hidebound legal maxims that law students learn is libel per se.

HER CUP RUNNETH OVER

After nearly thirty years in this business, I thought I had seen and heard everything. But Keshia Hemple takes the cake. We had a problem in the credit union. Keshia managed to get the credit union to make out cashier's checks in her name drawn from other employees' accounts. Naturally, after a month or so, when these employees got their monthly statements, they questioned these withdrawals. We conducted an investigation over the course of about three months and found Keshia had obtained money from twenty-nine separate accounts during that time. Our evidence was the canceled checks endorsed by Keshia.

Before she arrived in my office, I placed the canceled checks on my desk, so that they faced the chair where she would be sitting. When she came in, I pointed to the checks and said, "Here are all these checks. I suppose you know why I brought you here."

Keshia looked at them and with the most innocent face, replied, "No, I really don't know why you brought me in here. All I see are some checks with my name on them."

"Yes, that's true, but they weren't authorized by the account holder," I responded and then added, "I'm curious how you managed that."

"Oh, that wasn't difficult," she said.

I asked her to be a little more specific.

"Well, I just go down to the credit union and give someone else's name and number. Then I ask them to make out a cashier's check payable to me."

"How do you get their account number?" I asked.

"It's easy to find out an employee's credit union account number since it's the same as the employee's company number. Everybody wears their employee IDs, and every ID has the company number smack on it under the picture," she reminded me.

"Nailed!" I thought, patting myself on the back. "I not only have my evidence, I also have a verbal confession." Then I said, "You're in a lot of trouble, young lady."

Her response? "You don't think I intended to steal that money, do you?"

I couldn't wait to hear how she was going to try to weasel out of this, so I said, "Far be it from me to judge you. Even the Lord doesn't judge until the end. I'm not judging you as a person who steals, but you're gonna have a hell of a time explaining this to other people. We're talking about $8,000. Incidentally, Keisha, and I don't mean to pry, but what's going on if you weren't trying to steal the money?"

Without missing a beat, Keshia matter-of-factly said, "Well, I wanted to see whether or not you could get money out of other people's accounts. I was trying it out a lot of different times to see if any of the tellers would notice. Then, what I was gonna do was to write it up for the suggestion program and show how the credit union needs to have better security. Even though we wear our IDs, the tellers never ask us for them. As a matter of fact, they never even look at them. I thought if I could suggest that the tellers check the IDs, then . . . maybe . . . I could win an award."

I played along with her and said, "That probably would have been a good idea to turn in. Too bad you didn't put that on paper," I added, knowing full well she was handing me a line of crap.

"Well, I did!" she said, acting very excited.

"Right," I thought, "and your dog ate it and now you don't have it." But instead I said, "Well, I'd sure like to see it."

Then Keshia raised her voice and got even more excited. "You would!?" About this time, she started unbuttoning her blouse, not opening it wide or anything, but—right there in front of me—unhooking her bra in the middle and slipping her fingers inside one of the cups. It had a little pocket in it with a zipper. She unzipped it, reached in, and pulled out the suggestion form that she had completed in her own handwriting. I tried to keep my jaw steady as she handed it to me. It was a written confession. It said, "You've got a problem. I know it works cause I did it, and I got money twenty-nine times. It needs to be looked into. I think you should make the tellers check employee IDs."

I was dumbfounded. She was telling the truth! We didn't press criminal charges, but Keshia was terminated that day.

By the way, we implemented her suggestion immediately.

Panel Comments This case is reminiscent of the politician caught in the Abscam investigation a few years back. When asked why he took the money, he said he did it to conduct his own investigation into this corruption. Anyway, it's not surprising that some people do these things, but it's always surprising when they have such creative rationalizations. What's most astounding is when a plaintiff's attorney takes on a case like this. In this instance, we would guess the cause of action would be the denial of the suggestion award.

Legal Comments Under these circumstances, it is doubtful that the company would have any potential liability for discharging Keshia. However, the credit union may be liable for negligence if it does not obtain restitution from Keshia or otherwise replenish the employees' accounts from which withdrawals had been made.

4
THIEVES
AND
EMBEZZLERS

Petty? Sometimes. Blatant? Rarely. Ruthless? Occasionally. The most clever corporate criminals share the common characteristics of deception and greed. Unless the organization hires a staff of proactive security professionals, many white collar crimes can go undetected for years. Often an innocent or unrelated incident brought to the attention of a curious manager can ignite an investigation that leads to a startling discovery.

QUICK CHANGE

Mildred meekly stood beside Charlene's desk until Charlene noticed her presence. Charlene smiled warmly and asked, "Do you need something Mildred? How can I help you?"

Mildred set her mop and bucket down and responded, "Could I see Jackie, or is she too busy right now?"

Charlene was trying to read Mildred's expression. Mildred seemed calm, but it was quite uncharacteristic for her to have an urgent need to personally see the director of administration. Mildred usually communicated to Jackie through *Post-it* notes stuck to the phone when she'd finish cleaning Jackie's office.

"Jackie's currently working on a project, but I think she's alone in her office. Let me see if she can make herself available," Charlene responded politely. Charlene rang Jackie's extension and explained Mildred's need to see her. Then Charlene smiled and turned to Mildred, "Jackie says to come right in."

Mildred picked up her mop and bucket and walked into Jackie's office. Jackie greeted her enthusiastically. "Hi, Mildred, to what do I owe this unexpected visit?"

"Can I close the door, Jackie?"

"Sure, Mildred," Jackie responded as her brow began to wrinkle, "what's the matter?"

Mildred sat down in the chair facing Jackie and held steadfastly to her mop. Then she leaned across Jackie's desk and whispered, "Jackie, I think we have thieves among us."

"Thieves? Where? What's missing?"

"Toilet paper," Mildred intoned.

"Toilet paper, I see," Jackie returned with equal seriousness, holding back her inclination to giggle. "When did you start noticing this?"

"Several months ago," Mildred deadpanned.

"I see," Jackie encouraged.

"And that's not all, Jackie," Mildred added hushing her voice further.

"What do you mean, paper towels are missing, too?" Jackie asked, trying desperately to keep serious.

"Well, yes, those and some cleaning supplies are disappearing . . ."

"Mildred, how much are we talking about here?" Jackie interjected, growing somewhat impatient.

"About six cases of toilet paper over the past three months, a case or two of paper towels, three gallons of window cleaner, and two vacuum cleaners."

"Two vacuum cleaners!" Jackie responded, bolting up in her chair.

"Yes, they turned up missing this week."

Jackie felt guilty about her preliminary thoughts. This was serious. "Anything else, Mildred?"

"Yes, money is missing from the *Coke* machine."

"How can that be? Only the controller has the key, and you always give it back to him when you're refilling."

"I know, but you know he doesn't lock his desk at night. And that key is very easy to lift and return. It's just there for the taking," Mildred pointed out.

"I didn't know that," Jackie mused. "Well, Mildred, thank you for calling this to my attention. I'll investigate the situation, and hopefully we'll get it resolved."

The next day Jackie called a meeting of the six key managers and explained the problem. No one had a real clue as to who could be draining the *Coke* machine, much less pinching the *Charmin*. Most thought it was probably someone from the mail room staff, but they had no way of knowing for sure. The group agreed to hire an investigator. The investigator suggested that they install surveillance equipment in the vending area. To keep the installation secret from all nonmanagement employees, management told the employees the office would be closed on the weekend. The standard explanation was that the parking lot was being resealed, and major building maintenance was under way. No one was to come to the office. That weekend a video camera was installed in a strategic place, awaiting the culprit.

The management staff took turns reviewing the tape. During the week that followed, the managers observed employees engaged in such activities as scratching their privates, pulling their ears, jangling their change, or talking to themselves. The tape contained a continuous date and time stamp in the corner, and the screen typically ran black during off hours. On the fifth day, while fast forwarding through the black period, a manager noticed something unusual. At 4:55 A.M., a light flashed on showing a picture of the room. A moment later he observed Moriah, a trusted, eleven-year employee, enter the vending area. She was dressed in pearls and had her handbag and a key with her. She opened her bag, pulled out a pair of latex gloves, and put them on. She wiped the key off and inserted it in the *Coke* machine. When the door opened, she took the entire box of coins and dumped them in her bag. Then she carefully returned the coin box, relocked the door, left the vending area (apparently to return the key), came back to the room, removed the gloves, and turned off the light.

The reviewing manager immediately called Jackie. "Jackie, get down here right now."

"Did you get him?" she asked excitedly.

"Come see for yourself."

When Jackie reviewed the tape, she was stunned. She had known Moriah for years. Moriah was a great employee. She was always on time, she was rarely sick, she'd work overtime without a squawk, and her work was impeccable. Jackie was beside herself. The hardest part was to show the tape to Moriah's manager, Sue Ellen. Sue Ellen would be heartbroken. As Jackie suspected, when

Sue Ellen viewed the tape, her eyes flooded as she saw Moriah don her rubber gloves.

"Jackie, how am I going to handle this? I don't even want to look at her. How could she do such a thing? I just gave her an excellent performance review and authorized a substantial salary increase," she wailed. "I just can't face her now—I just can't, Jackie. You're going to have to help me."

"You won't have to, Sue Ellen," Jackie assured her. "I've already spoken to our outside counsel. He's drawn up a release that says we'll agree not to prosecute her if she reimburses the company for our costs to install the video equipment. And of course, she'll be terminated today. I've arranged for Charlene to have her in my office when I return. I'll show her the tape and give her the release. In the meantime, clean out her desk and have it ready for Charlene. Moriah will not return to the work area."

"Oh, thanks, Jackie, I knew I couldn't deal with this one."

Jackie met with Moriah as planned. Moriah was very embarrassed and quickly agreed to the release. Jackie also presented her with the bill for the video equipment and informed Moriah that payment would be due in fifteen days. The matter was settled and Moriah was whisked out.

Although the company had no hard evidence, they suspected Moriah was also responsible for the missing supplies and equipment. Her husband, Stan, conveniently ran his own cleaning business.

About a week later, Moriah's husband called Jackie. "Jackie, this is Stan, Moriah's husband. I want to know something. Since we're paying for this video equipment, do we get to keep it? I think we should."

Jackie was so shocked by his gall that before she could contain herself, she blurted, "Keep it!?! Keep it!?! Noooo, you don't get to keep it, you idiot. You're lucky we let you keep your thieving wife's butt out of jail!"

Panel Comments   Because of costly and time-consuming litigation, corporations are often reluctant to prosecute "white collar" criminals. Consequently, some companies have started to use the peer panel process as an alternative. Here co-workers are selected to determine the appropriate treatment of the accused. These panels review the case and develop effective ways to deal with the crimes that impact their business.

Legal Comments   The surreptitious surveillance of employees in the workplace is fraught with risk. Certain federal laws and many state statutes prohibit or regulate an employer's right to monitor their employees' conduct through electronic means. Even in those states that do not have a specific statute, employees are likely to have claims for invasion of privacy. Any surveillance, monitoring of telephone conversations or the like, should be carefully reviewed with counsel who is familiar with laws in the affected jurisdiction *before* the surveillance is implemented.

GHOST RIDERS

"Sanford Cooper," Sanford responded automatically as he answered his phone.

"Mr. Cooper, this is Marty Howell, owner of Howell's Gifts in Needham. I'm calling really more out of curiosity than anything else. I'm not a customer, so this doesn't have anything to do with your products."

"What seems to be the problem, Mr. Howell?" Sanford asked calmly.

"There's no real problem. There's this recurring incident involving your company, which seems a might peculiar. I thought maybe you'd want to look into it, just to be on the safe side," Marty responded.

Sanford had no idea where this was leading. His prior experience as a detective taught him to combine instinct with good old fashioned investigative techniques. Right now his instincts were telling him he'd better really listen. When a local business owner calls about something involving the company "out of curiosity," there is probably more to the story than the shopowner's concern.

"Well, Mr. Howell, you certainly have my interest piqued," Sanford encouraged.

"Let's see," Marty began, "it started about two years ago. About once a month, around the twentieth or so, a woman by the name of Jane Smith cashes one of your company checks for $500 at my store."

"Do you have any trouble clearing the checks?" Sanford asked.

"Oh, no, that's not it. What makes it seem so strange is that these are not ordinary payroll checks. They're drafts. I don't know why she picked my store, except maybe we have a liberal check cashing policy and do a large volume of business. She always buys some small gift items, generally amounting to under $50, and keeps the remaining cash."

"Hmmm," Sanford thought, "a draft suggests that the woman is cashing claim payments. I can understand that claim payments might come in the form of installments— but for two years? Gee, even large settlements are made in lump sums. Let's see, sometimes in long-term rehabilitation cases, drafts are issued to make claim payments for reimbursement of medical expense, but that seems unlikely in this case."

Then he said aloud, "Mr. Howell, could you do me a favor?"

"If I can. What do you need?" Marty responded.

"Do you still happen to have the last draft Jane Smith cashed at your store?"

"As a matter of fact, I've already put it through for deposit. But I made a copy of it before calling you."

"Great, could you fax me your copy?"

"Sure, what's your fax number?"

He rattled off the fax number and said, "Thank you so much for taking the time to share this information. I'll look into it. If there's more to this than meets the eye, will you be willing to talk with us further?"

"Oh, sure, no problem. We're all in business to survive. We have to help each other."

"Thanks again, Mr. Howell," and Sanford clicked off.

Before Sanford had a chance to fully reflect on the notes from his telephone conversation, John, his secretary, walked in with the fax. "This just came for you, Sanford."

"Thanks, John."

When he reviewed the fax he said to himself, "It's a company claim draft all right." Then he immediately called the internal auditors and asked them to investigate. Within two weeks, Sanford learned that Jane Smith had been issued claim checks amounting to $27,500 for fifty-five separate auto claims. The auditors also discovered that these claim checks went back four years. The first two years they had been cashed at a different gift store in the same neighborhood.

The audit also revealed that Jane Smith was the wife of Felix Hanson. Felix was a respected, high-performing employee for twenty-two years. Felix was also a supervisor of an *auto claims unit.* The auditors discovered Felix's clever embezzlement technique that eventually led to his prosecution and conviction. Felix would alter a claim report developed by one of his adjustors by retyping it. The new report would indicate that there was a passenger in the car. The passenger listed was always Jane Smith, his wife's maiden name. As supervisor of the unit, Felix had certain claims payment authority, so he would add a memo to the file, which said, "Get a release and pay her off so we don't get sued." These files, along with hundreds and hundreds of others, would be processed by a variety of different data entry operators each month. If it had not been for Marty Howell's healthy curiosity, Felix might have been able to continue his scam until retirement.

 We applaud Sanford's quick action and good judgment.

Panel Comments

Sanford's decision to call in the auditors to investigate was prudent. However, it would Legal Comments have been equally prudent to contact legal counsel, because company investigations that inadvertently violate an employee's rights may jeopardize a subsequent criminal prosecution.

A CLEAN CASE OF CORRUPTION

Ty Ross was, in his day, one of the company's most notorious criminals. He ruled a well-organized staff of three hundred through intimidation and payoffs. His knowledge of the company structure and procedures, plus friends at the top, gave him all he needed to bury his misdeeds deep within corporate headquarters. No one crossed Ty.

Ty began his career with a series of small-time rip offs. He soloed his first jobs by knocking off unsuspecting sanitary napkin machines in the ladies' restrooms. With forty-two restrooms to service, he was able to amass over $5,000 (in nickels and dimes!) before his discovery. When the feminine products company's distributor complained, a brief investigation led to Ty as the culprit. Normally, an employee caught in a criminal activity is no longer covered by the bonding company and is removed from the job. In Ty's case, however, the firm's bonding company was required to pay off the feminine products distributor for their loss, and Ty retained his job. No one challenged the decision.

At the time, the company had no internal security force, and the human resources manager was too weak to stand up against the vice president of administration, who somehow managed to convince the president that Ty should be kept on staff. The vice president claimed it was the company's moral obligation to work with troubled employees and attempt to assist in their rehabilitation. (We later learn this plea was self-serving.) So, strange as it seems, Ty not only kept his position but also did not make restitution for the money stolen from the vending machine. Subsequently, Ty became a model employee, and the incident was forgotten. Several years later, he was promoted to supervisor of maintenance.

Ty's staff was responsible for maintenance of four major buildings in the complex. With all his experience in maintenance, Ty had no problem padding the staffing needs. With the excess staff, Ty constructed a clandestine maintenance organization whose sole purpose was to provide outside cleaning service. He made sales calls and set up contracts with other local companies and organizations within a forty-mile radius. He took teams of company employees, using company equipment and supplies, and serviced his customers. Those teams received their regular paycheck, plus a "bonus" for the outside jobs. Once they accepted the hush money, Ty had them for life. All remaining profits were shared between Ty and a silent partner.

Ty's business flourished over the years as he accrued more and more customers. Fortunately, some unrelated incidents led to his eventual exposure. Ty had a weakness for women.

When Dirk Danby, a new human resources manager who was unaware of Ty's history, received six letters from female employees complaining about sexual harassment, an investigation ensued. While Dirk was investigating the sexual harassment complaint, subtle comments about the side business caused Dirk to dig deeper. Further probing revealed the scope of Ty's enterprise. The evidence suggested—though it couldn't be proven directly—that he was in cahoots with the vice president of administration, the real mastermind of the operation.

Dirk approached Ty with the letters and asked him to respond to the complaints. Dirk never accused Ty but told him to go home that night and think about how he would respond. The next morning, Ty met with Dirk. Ty denied the allegations, saying the letters were simply not true and he couldn't respond.

Dirk pointed out that if Ty couldn't help defend his case and it went to trial, it would be his word against the six women.

Ty decided to resign.

In spite of the additional knowledge Dirk had about Ty's activities, he carried him on the payroll for seven extra weeks in order to protect his pension. Subsequently, Dirk launched a full scale investigation of the vice president of administration. Dirk felt the vice president was the real cause of the problem, and the cleaning business was only the tip of the iceberg. He was correct.

Panel Comments Human Resources is often asked to "draw the line" on what is acceptable use of company materials and facilities, and upper management often prefers to look the other way. To effectively get management's attention, human resources managers should verify and present the cost of such violations to the key decision makers.

Legal Comments Dirk Danby appears to have handled both the sex harassment complaint and Ty's blatant misconduct appropriately. One suggestion is to consider obtaining a release from employees in these situations. Carefully-drafted releases can play an important role in minimizing an employer's legal exposure and help secure the prompt dismissal of claims rather than force the employer to incur the cost and inconvenience of full-fledged trials.

5
BUMBLERS, BIMBOS, AND BUFFOONS

Perhaps every manager's worst nightmare is to make a careless error that results in a disastrous mistake. Professionals work hard to avoid these terrors by maintaining a constant vigil against severe errors in judgment. Occasionally they fail at their mission and face the dragon of their own human imperfections. Then there are those charming, good-natured souls who lack common sense. Errors in judgment and foul-ups are second nature to them. Although these employees may be able to sneak through a job interview by overcompensating with delightful interpersonal skills, their day-to-day job performance always reveals the truth.

THE IDEAL CANDIDATE

Ted sat back in his chair and smiled. Finding the right individual to manage the Research Department required a person with scientific knowledge as well as leadership skills. The whole interview process was both arduous and draining. This morning, however, Ted felt as though the fog had lifted. He finally made his decision. The ideal candidate emerged after screening over one hundred applications and interviewing nearly fifteen candidates. It was during the fourth interview that Ted knew it. Within the first few minutes, Ted knew Mark was perfect for the job. Ted was ready to offer Mark the job on the spot, but he dutifully interviewed the remaining candidates to keep himself honest. In the end, Mark was his man. There was no doubt about it. Not only were Mark's references sterling, but he also outdistanced all the other candidates so dramatically that Ted didn't even have a backup for consideration. He secretly prayed Mark would accept as he called to make the offer.

"Research, Mark speaking," the voice responded, somewhat hoarsely.

"Mark, this is Ted Fenton calling. Are you okay? You sound terrible."

"Oh, I'm much better than I sound. It's just a cold. I'm sure I'll have my regular voice back in a few days."

"Are you still interested in the position with us?" Ted asked, tapping his pen nervously on his desk.

"You bet!" Mark responded enthusiastically.

"Great! We'd like to offer the position at $54,000. You can take the weekend to think about it if you'd like, but I'd appreciate your getting back to me on Monday with your decision and let us know what . . . ."

"I don't need the weekend," Mark interrupted. "The answer is yes. I can start in two weeks. I'll give notice today if you'll fax me a confirmation letter with the particulars. We have a fax in our department, and everyone is out to lunch until 1:30. Can you get your secretary to do it within the hour?"

"Sure, no problem," Ted responded, thrilled that he'd have this thing wrapped up before the weekend.

"Great," Mark said. "Today is Friday the fifth, so I guess I'll see you Monday the twenty-second."

"Terrific," Ted said. "Report to the Human Resources Department, and someone will bring you up to my office. I'll see you then."

"Boy, am I glad this is over with," Ted thought as he walked over to his secretary's desk with Mark's file. He told her to send the standard offer letter and handed her a slip with the annual salary and start date.

"It will be so great to have Mark heading the department. I can't wait until he gets here," Ted said over his shoulder as he returned to his office and relaxed behind his desk. After a moment, he stood up, scooped up the stack of resumes and applications littering his desk, and triumphantly dropped them in the trash.

Two weeks later, Joan Cutter, the human resources manager, arrived at Ted's office with Mark. Ted's secretary was away from her desk, so Joan tapped lightly on Ted's door. Ted looked up at Joan and then at the gentlemen who stood beside her. A puzzled look crossed his face.

Joan recognized that something was awry, but she began anyway. "Ted, I've brought Mark Simmons up for his orientation. How would you like to get started?"

Ted coughed nervously and extended his hand. "Mark . . . welcome aboard. We're . . . uh . . . so glad to have you," he stuttered. "Mark . . . uh . . . uhm . . . could you excuse us a moment, please? I'll be with you shortly. We've got a slight crisis on our hands with . . . uh . . . um . . . one of our government contractors. I'm sure I won't be long," Ted said as he ushered Mark out of his office to a waiting area across the hall.

Ted sped back to his office and closed the door. Still gripping the door handle, he slumped against the door and started to grow pale.

"What is it, Ted?" Joan asked with sincere concern. "Are you ill?"

"Christ, Joan, this isn't the guy I hired. I hired a different person. I know this fellow's name is Mark, but he's not the guy I wanted. How the hell did this happen?"

Ted was starting to develop visible drops of perspiration above his lip as Joan responded. "Our paperwork indicated you hired Mark Simmons. This is Mark Simmons. Here's a copy of the offer letter and his file."

Ted looked at the file, flipping through the application and resume. The papers rattled in his quaking hands. Then Ted's whole body began to shake. He started to pace and let out a howl as he knocked his knee on an arm chair. He raced to his desk and started fumbling through his papers. Then he remembered he had thrown out all the resumes. He looked at Mark Simmons' file again and began to put the pieces together. The sudden realization caused him to slide slowly and limply into his desk chair. "How could I have been so stupid?" First he looked befuddled and distraught, then his demeanor assumed a catatonic quality.

Joan was really growing concerned. She stared at him awkwardly and finally broke the silence.

"Look, Ted, could you be a little more specific? I'll see what I can do to help you."

"There's nothing you can do. I screwed up. I just plumb screwed up. I don't know how I'm going to deal with this."

"Deal with what?"

"The guy I intended to hire was a different man. His name was Mark *Simon,* not Simmons. When I called *this* Mark with the offer, I must've picked up the wrong file. He had a cold when I called, so I didn't notice the difference in voice. I was so excited when he accepted that I just handed the papers to Sue to type an offer letter. She handled the rest and I forgot about it. Joan, I don't know how to say this, but the guy sitting out there is the last person I would hire. He's a total jerk—and a weirdo on top of it. He's okay technically, but during the interview he started preaching all this religious stuff to me and asked me about my church and being saved. We are in deep shit here."

Joan was stunned. She could usually solve problems, but this one was a doozy.

"It's not like I can say, 'Whoops, sorry we offered you the job by mistake. You can go back to your cult or wherever you came from.' I mean Joan, this guy resigned from a perfectly good job. I'm stuck, I tell you, stuck! I've just hired the employee from hell!" he gasped, fearing what loomed ahead.

Ted *was* stuck. Joan quickly assessed that the only way out of this one was a major settlement, which the company could not afford. They were going to have to make the best of it. "Tell you what, Ted, I'll reschedule part of his orientation until you can collect yourself. Then we'll pow wow on how to approach this realistically."

"Fine, Joan, whatever you say. Just get him out of here until I figure out what to do."

Joan made some excuses to Mark about a temporary research crisis that required Ted's immediate attention and caused a schedule change. She ushered Mark down the hall and sent him to the Benefits Department to sign papers and get acquainted with health and life coverages. When Joan returned to Ted's office, she noticed that the color had returned to his face and he seemed drier above the lip. He was fumbling with a paper clip when it slipped from his hand and flew across the room. Joan coughed quietly to let him know of her presence.

"Okay, here's our strategy," she began, "you have to give this guy a chance to do the job. You've got to be professional one hundred percent of the way. However, you have to follow policy to the letter and document any performance issues, conversations, everything. If he's as bad as you say, he'll write his own ticket, and he'll be gone at little cost to us within ninety days. Now I know that this means you won't be able to delegate the new Fragmore research project to him. Since we don't have any other reasonable alternatives, you'll just have to honcho the project yourself, at least for the next three months. That's the best I can come up with."

Joan's strategy worked. Mark created a series of disruptive incidents, one of which involved clipping passages from the Bible and putting them on employees' desks. Ted counseled and warned Mark that his behavior was inappropriate. Ted also pointed out that the company had a 'no distribution, no solicitation' policy, which meant that only company-approved literature could be circulated in the workplace.

Fortunately for Ted, Mark ignored these warnings. Mark continued to disseminate religious literature. Employees complained that Mark was harassing them with his constant barrage of religious pamphlets. He also cornered co-workers during breaks and lunch and launched into intense discussions about religious philosophy. If they didn't agree with his views, Mark would assure them that he would pray for them. As each week progressed, Mark walled in his work station with religious pictures and symbols. He attempted to snare passersby to discuss his fondness for these religious objects. After repeated verbal and written warnings, Ted fired Mark. The mission was accomplished in less than sixty days, and Ted's blood pressure returned to normal.

 This is a classic example of why an employ-**Panel Comments** ment offer should always come from the Human Resources Department. Too many

things—compensation packages, health and welfare benefits, and relocation plans—can be misunderstood. When
this happens, the employee feels deceived or cheated,
which can sour the employment relationship from the start.

An additional precaution against mis-hiring is to make an
offer contingent on the successful completion of a physical.
This gives the company one last chance to check out the
candidate before he or she leaves his current employment.

Joan and Ted's concern over potential legal
repercussions if Mark had been denied
Legal Comments employment was justified. Such a decision
could well have led Mark to sue the company, alleging that
the offer was fraudulent or the company was negligent and
that he suffered serious damage by losing his former
position.

In addition, this story presents a potential issue of
discrimination on the basis of religious belief. While it
appears that Mark went overboard, an employee may not
be discharged or harassed because of his religion and is
entitled to some flexibility in expressing his views about
religion in the workplace. The company had a duty to
accommodate his religious beliefs. But if Mark began to
interfere with operations, annoyed co-workers by
proselytizing, or engaged in similar conduct, the company
would not be legally obligated to continue to employ him
indefinitely.

THROWING YOUR BRAINS OUT WITH THE TRASH

Forrest McHugh was beaming. Employees filed into the auditorium, greeting each other in hushed tones and friendly handshakes. Once everyone was settled, the stage crew dimmed the house lights and trailed Forrest with a spotlight as he approached the podium.

"Welcome to our first employee meeting in our beautiful new building and high tech auditorium." The sound quality was terrific—no microphone squeals—and everyone was attentive.

"You've all worked hard to help us achieve this success. We are so fortunate to have moved to this sparkling new facility in the northwest sector of the city. It's through your hard work and effort that we've been able to move from the grim, grey factory district to an open environment, surrounded by real trees and real flowering plants. The architects and interior designers have done an outstanding job, and I hope that you are as proud and happy to be here as I am."

The crowed buzzed in agreement, while Forrest paused. "It's because we're all so proud of our new environment that I feel we must talk about maintaining that pride. We had a tendency—myself included—to be somewhat careless in our prior facility. Never careless in our work, mind you, but careless about our surroundings. If coffee spilled, we didn't bother to wipe it up. There was often a trail of popcorn that led from the vending machines to some of your desk areas. Our contract cleaning crew was not very effective, and dust bunnies occasionally hopped about when someone left the door ajar and a strong wind whipped through the main floor. We were all so intense about helping this company grow that we didn't pay much attention to our environment. I guess it was pretty hard to see very well in the dismal setting, so it's not surprising none of us looked very hard. But we've moved uptown now, and I'm sure you'll join me in treating this office as though it were your home. You've earned it and deserve to enjoy it for a long, long time."

Forrest smiled and paused as he panned the audience. "To insure that we continually enjoy our new surroundings, I've hired an excellent cleaning service. But I'm also asking each and every one of you to do your part to help maintain the building. If you see a stray piece of paper on the floor, pitch in and help us keep our company beautiful. I, for one, will make it my business to tour the halls on a regular basis and contribute to this ideal. I appreciate your cooperation. I hope you are as thrilled as I am and will join me and Mayor Clemson, as well as your favorite Channel 8 news personalities, in the dedication ceremonies and ribbon cutting. With that in mind, please adjourn to our cafeteria for the ceremony and refreshments."

The houselights brightened and everyone began their exit. The activities and social period lasted about an hour, and employees returned to their work stations to complete the last hour or so of the day.

Ozzie had always been known as a practical joker. He was overweight, balding, and full of mischief. His favorite hangout was *Spencer Gifts*, checking out the latest gag that he could pull on his co-workers. Ozzie helped make the three years they worked in the factory district's dismal dungeon somewhat tolerable. So, when he stepped off the elevator clutching his chest and falling to the floor, everyone just laughed and walked over him on their way back to their desk. A few looked back, shaking their heads.

"Ozzie will do anything for a laugh," Larry chuckled, but his smile abruptly changed to horror. "Oh, God, Ozzie is really having a heart attack. He's vomiting and gasping for air." In a flash, he directed Dick, "Quick, get some paper towels, I've got to administer CPR." Then he yelled to Marcy, "Call 911."

Dick was a fairly new employee, who was about nineteen years old, and worked in the mail room. He ran to the restroom while Larry was loosening Ozzie's collar. Ozzie was unconscious by this time, and Larry was listening for breath and a heartbeat. Dick promptly arrived with the paper towels. Larry was working on Ozzie and had his hand extended for the paper towels. Instead of handing the towels to Larry so that he could clear Ozzie's air passage, Dick immediately started cleaning the rug.

"What the hell are you doing, you moron?" Larry screamed as the seconds ticked by and panic was setting in.

"Cleaning the rug. Forrest said we needed to take pride in the building," Dick replied earnestly.

"Jesus Christ, give me the goddamn towels and get the hell out of here!" Larry bellowed and worked feverishly until the paramedics arrived.

Panel Comments Beware of the "literal" order taker! We'd give Dick a score of one hundred for effort and dedication and zero for results. He'd be great in a monotonous job that no one else would do.

OFF CENTER

Rosalind reviewed the budget figures from last month, penciled a line through the numbers that were being changed, and noted the changes in the margins. When she was finished, she handed the copy to her secretary, Bambi.

"Bambi, please arrange to have this ready for me by this afternoon. We'll need to send it to duplicating along with some other materials I'll be working on. Everything must be put together by 11:00 A.M. tomorrow. It's important that the meeting attendees have the information before our 2:00 P.M. meeting."

"Be glad to, Rosalind. I'll certainly do my best," Bambi replied in her usual sunny manner.

Bambi began working for Rosalind about five weeks ago. She was marvelous with clients, and everyone in the office seemed to like her. She was positive, upbeat, and always had a cheerful word. She never got involved in the office gossip—a plus in a public relations firm. Rosalind did notice that Bambi required a bit of hand-holding on instructions, and it seemed to take her longer to catch on to some of the more basic office practices than Rosalind thought should be necessary. On this particular day, one of Rosalind's staffers dropped by her office while she was locked away preparing for tomorrow's meeting.

"Rosalind," Jack asked, "how is Bambi getting along these days?"

"Slow," Rosalind sighed, "but she's so dedicated and works so hard, I really think I just need to give her a little more time to catch on. Besides, she really is a pleasure to have around. Why do you ask?"

"Well, I've been observing her periodically during the past three hours, and I think you ought to see this."

"What?"

"Just come see," Jack smiled as he attempted to restrain himself.

They stood about fifteen feet behind Bambi. Rosalind noticed that the budget she had assigned to Bambi was in the typewriter, but it had been inserted on a diagonal. She looked at Jack, shaking her head and shrugging her shoulders. Then she walked up to Bambi, just as Bambi removed the paper from the machine.

"There, finally done," Bambi said proudly, "with time to spare so we can make it to duplicating. I'll tell ya, this was one tough job, getting those numbers in at just the right angle!" she exclaimed, sporting a wide grin. Her eyes sparkled as she handed the budget to Rosalind.

Rosalind thanked her and walked back in her office with Jack close behind.

"Close the door, Jack," Rosalind said under her breath.

Jack jumped up and obliged.

For the past three hours, Bambi had taken Rosalind's original budget sheet and retyped it with all the old numbers. Then Bambi typed over the old numbers with hyphens to show they had been crossed out. Next, she reinserted the paper on a diagonal to type in Rosalind's new numbers to make sure she could get them at "just the right angle."

"I can't believe this. I just can't believe this. No one is this dumb—no one."

Jack returned a devilish smile as if to say, "Well, yes, I think there is, and you have her working for you."

Panel Comments All of this could have been avoided if the company had used an effective secretarial testing package to screen out unqualified candidates. These tests involve not only standard skills assessment—such as typing speed and accuracy, grammar and punctuation ability, and general office procedures—

but also decision-making capabilities. The employee's ability to set priorities and demonstrate clear decisions can be measured through a series of "in-box" exercises. If Bambi had been administered this battery, the results would no doubt reveal that she was incapable of meeting the essential demands of the job.

6
SNAKES
AND VILLAINS

S elf-serving creatures silently slither or gnaw
their way into corporations. They hide their
vicious nature with well-crafted charm.
Paranoia fuels them, and immorality sustains them.
Without remorse, these clever varmints go
undetected for years as they burrow into company
coffers or destroy the reputation of others. The
most savvy often reach responsible positions,
building their careers on lies, treachery, or
corruption. They save their skin by shedding it of
screw-ups or venomously biting co-workers with
blame. Misdeeds are camouflaged in a dense grass
of paperwork, then carried off to tunnels of
deception. Along the way, they leave droppings of
insensitivity and pure meanness. Unfortunately, it
takes more than a few applications of *D-Con* to
eradicate these vermin.

INSURING HIS GUILT

Alan reviewed his calendar. Skylar Thomas was due any minute. Although Skylar had been around for years, Alan seldom worked with him. Skylar was recently promoted to a high-profile position, vice president of corporate responsibility, making sure the corporation contributed to the well-being of the community through appropriate recycling. He frequently made public speeches on behalf of the company and had become somewhat of a local media darling.

Skylar's responsibilities also put him in charge of a spin-off division that salvaged cars, furniture, and other saleable materials that were acquired through repossession. He had to insure that non-saleable items were disposed of in an environmentally sound manner.

Alan's secretary buzzed him to let him know that Skylar was on the way in. Alan rose from his desk and extended his hand as Skylar approached.

"Hi, Sky, how are you?"

"Oh, running here and everywhere, making sure this company stays on its toes," he grinned.

Skylar was a handsome man. His stature was impressive, and he carried himself with a confidence that others admired. He had a certain flair for giving the illusion that he came from a wealthy background. Occasionally, some of the executives commented that Skylar seemed to be living higher than his salary should allow, but they brushed this off with unsubstantiated talk that his family had money.

"How can I help you today?" Alan asked.

"Well, Alan, I think I've got a problem with my manager of the Salvage Center."

"Are we talking about Clint Lockmore?"

"Yes, Clint Lockmore. Then you know him?" Skylar queried.

Alan nodded. He had known Clint for nearly twenty-five years. Clint was one of the straightest arrows he'd ever met.

"Let me fill you in on the details," Skylar offered. "Unfortunately, we had to close down a gun shop out in Boca. The guns were all shipped up here, and there seemed to be a discrepancy with the bill of lading. They were supposed to ship us 741 firearms. Clint claims the carrier shorted us by 29 items."

"What makes you think Clint is involved?"

"The guy is sloppy. He's been short on other inventory items, but it's been small potatoes. I've never really worried too much about it until now. These shortages always seem to occur with out-of-state shipments. Clint informs me that the shippers short us, and then he files an insurance claim against them. He never seems to make a claim twice with the same shipper, and they've always reimbursed us for the loss. It's just that I'm starting to get suspicious. The missing firearms have a retail value of $12,720. Now that's a hefty sum."

"And another thing," Skylar continued, "none of the other missing items was really traceable. But these firearms all have serial numbers, so at least we have a place to start."

"Do you have the serial numbers with you?"

"You bet I do," Skylar smiled and handed him the list.

"Well, I'll look into this, Sky, and keep you informed of the progress."

"I hope you nail that bastard. I've been wanting to fire the incompetent jackass for months now."

Skylar got up, and Alan walked him to the door.

"Don't worry, Sky, we'll get to the bottom of this," Alan assured him.

Alan walked back to his desk thinking, "This is very strange. Very strange, indeed."

Alan was an avid bow hunter, and so was Clint. Occasionally, he would see Clint on the range for target practice. Sometimes they'd have a beer together after they finished rounds. The most vivid recollection of these encounters was one day when Clint got very upset. It was two days before gun season was about to open.

"Damn gun hunters," Clint railed, "they aren't sportsmen. I hate guns—all forms of them. I don't even keep one in my home. I'd be worried to death with my kids around."

Alan had that conversation with Clint eight years ago. Something was not right about this case, but Alan went forward and interviewed Clint. The discussion raised more questions than it answered. He ruled Clint out as a suspect, but the missing guns remained a mystery.

Forty-five days into the investigation, Alan received an anonymous phone call. A muffled female voice said, "Call Skylar's insurance agent, Ralph Denver, if you want to find out the real truth about the firearms," and the phone clicked.

Alan pulled out his yellow pages and located the Denver and Crylon Agency. He asked for Denver's assistant.

"This is Alice Edleman. How can I help you?"

Carefully wording his introduction, Alan began, "Ms. Edleman, I'm Alan Comptom, vice president of corporate security for the Sussex Street Lending Association. There were some items taken from one of our employee's office. There appears to be some discrepancy as to whether his homeowners policy covers the items or whether our company insurance will have to absorb the loss. Can you check his policy to see if these items are covered?"

"Sure, what is the policyholder's name?" she asked.

"Skylar Thomas."

"What type of items?"

"Firearms."

"What kind of firearms?"

"Rifles and handguns."

"How many does he have?"

"About a couple dozen."

"Well, I can tell you right now, that sounds like a major gun collection to me. Items like that wouldn't be covered by his regular policy. We'd have to prepare a special rider to insure full coverage."

"Would you mind checking his policy to see if he's made any recent changes to provide for extended coverage?"

"I'll be glad to." Ms. Edleman put Alan on hold, and Alan's heart raced as he waited for her to return to the line. The piped-in commerical-on-hold, which told of the wonderful service Denver and Crylon offered their customers, didn't offer much distraction.

Ms. Edleman returned to the line. "Mr. Compton, you're off the hook. He's covered. He called this change in about a month ago."

"Bingo!" Alan silently cheered and then coolly asked, "Could we just match our serial numbers to be sure we're talking about the same items?"

"No problem." She rattled off twenty-nine serial numbers. They were a perfect match.

"That bastard," Alan thought. "I'm going to get his miserable ass."

"Oh, one more thing, Ms. Edlemen. So I can put this thing to rest, could you fax me a copy of the change request and the endorsement? Our number is 522-1279."

"Sure, what department?"

"Corporate Security."

"You'll have it in five minutes."

"Thanks, Ms. Edleman. You've been a terrific help."

Alan's private fax sat on his credenza. It couldn't hum out the evidence fast enough for him. Alan's excitement grew with each page that spewed forth. Then he called the vice president of human resources, Sam Chapman.

"Sam, you know the firearm's case I've been working on. Well, I've got our man. And you're not going to believe this." Alan revealed his evidence.

"We've got to get the president involved in this one," Sam said immediately. "He's close to this guy, and we can't do anything without his knowledge. There are all sorts of implications with this one. I'd like to string him up, but I'm afraid we're not going to be able to do that."

"Here's what I suggest," Sam continued. "I know Harrison is in board meetings all day, but they all go home tonight. Call Julie and tell her to schedule Harrison for a 6:00 P.M. emergency meeting. I'll meet you there. In the meantime, I'll inform Nate Feinstein from Corporate Counsel and have him join us. This is going to be a real hot potato."

The four sealed themselves off in the private study of the president's suite. This was the first that Harrison had heard of the investigation. When Alan presented the evidence of Skylar's twisted plan, Harrison turned ashen.

"We have to be very careful," Harrison said. "Skylar has tremendous visibility in the community. We can't let this out. How would it look to the world if our vice president of corporate responsibility turned out to be a crook? We don't need that kind of publicity."

Nate had drafted a solution. "Look Harrison, we have him dead in the water. The guy has an ego that won't quit. I know we can't afford to let the world know about this, but neither can he. I suggest that we present him with the evidence and ask him to resign. I'll prepare a document and get him to sign off on any claims against us, and we'll agree not to prosecute him. Then you issue a memo in your usual style and state that he's taking early retirement."

They all agreed that Nate's suggestion was the best approach. The next day, Sam, Alan, and Nate met with Skylar. Skylar looked around the room and seemed unaffected by the other's presence.

"Sky, we've solved our case. You won't have to worry about Clint any more," Alan said.

"That's terrific," smiled Skylar, continuing with his charade. "So who's the bad guy?"

"I'm afraid it's you, Sky," Alan smiled triumphantly.

"Me! What do you mean?" Skylar responded, looking genuinely shocked.

After Alan presented the evidence, Nate handed Skylar a pen to sign the release of claims. Embarrassed and defeated, Skylar signed off without an argument. Then, Alan escorted Skylar to his office to clean out his things.

While in Skylar's office, Alan observed Norma. Norma, a long-time employee, had become Skylar's executive assistant when he was promoted to vice president. She seemed deeply absorbed in her work. The bond between her and her PC was so strong that she never even looked up from her desk when the moving crew walked out with a dolly stacked with boxes of Skylar's personal belongings.

Alan asked Skylar to wait at the freight elevator with the movers for just a moment. He said he needed to give Norma some instructions on how to handle this untimely exit.

Alan stood in front of Norma's desk and cleared his throat to get her attention. She swung around in her chair and faced him. "Hello, Alan."

"Norma, I need to tell you something highly confidential. Skylar has decided to take early retirement. The announcement will come out of the president's office tomorrow morning. Please cancel his appointments for the rest of the day, and take messages from any callers. Simply tell them he is currently unavailable."

Norma just nodded her head and never said a word. Then she smiled a knowing, satisfied smile and returned to her PC.

Sky's sudden resignation without the usual fanfare did raise some executive eyebrows, but no one really knew the circumstances. About three months later, the scuttlebutt filtering through mahogany row was that Skylar was emerging from retirement to become a public servant of sorts. Within the week, Skylar appeared on the front page of the daily newspaper, shaking the hand of the mayor. He'd been invited to sit on the board of a public utility. His major responsibility was to act as one of the watchdogs over their multi-million dollar budget!

Panel Comments Unfortunately, allowing a nasty crook to go free because exposure would create a "public relations problem" is an attractive option, at least for the short term. However, it's ethically indefensible, especially in light of the fact that this crook's intention was to pin his crime on an innocent person. Additionally, the long-term public relations perspective may not be so attractive and is ethically suspect. This individual may well be publicly exposed at a later date, and the company's part in the earlier "hush solution" could come back to haunt them.

Legal Comments Never overlook the complainant as the possible wrongdoer. The long-term salutary results Alan achieved confirms that a professional response to problems is worth the effort and short-term inconvenience of a thorough investigation before the course of action is determined.

HAVING HER DAY IN COURT

Early in my career I was assigned to the adjutant general's office. I made the big mistake of thinking that the frazzled, ill-tempered legal staff would behave like all other bureaucrats when it came to following personnel policies. Looking back at how much the feds drained this poor, dedicated bunch, I suppose I could hardly blame them for making a mockery of our silly rules. These attorneys were required to toil in a rare niche of public service that could squeeze sweat out of the tundra. To them, asking for compliance with internal procedures was akin to requesting them to dirty their hands in non-recyclable administrative garbage.

So when Dawn Collins filed an appeal that her "satisfactory" performance rating should have been higher, I went by the book. With a quadruplicate set of Employee Complaint Form Number 9857 in hand, I eagerly met with her boss, Chief Counsel Chet Jantzen. I asked him to prepare a succinct defense of his rating, so it could fit neatly in the space labeled "supervisor's response."

I explained that I would retain the original, and the remaining copies would go to the three-person panel who would review the case. All this was prescribed by the "Appeals Section" of the agency's *Personnel Policies Manual.* I proudly produced a photocopy of the "Appeals Section" so Chet would know I had done my homework.

As I watched him review the section, it didn't occur to me that the gleam in his eye might reflect more than the chrome from his desk lamp. (It's only after I gained experience that I learned to read the fine points of these signs. Today I'd know that gleam was a glint, guaranteeing that trouble would follow as surely as a bail bondsman's goons pursue a "skip.") Unfortunately, this was only my second human resources job. If I had some clue about what the staff was plotting, I might have averted the forthcoming disaster. I was certainly not prepared for the legal gang-bang Chet and his cronies had in store for poor Dawn.

My first inkling that something was awry came when I stopped by Chet's office. I asked him when he thought he'd finish completing his form, so I could send it on to the panel.

"I've just about got all my witnesses lined up," he grinned.

"Witnesses, what witnesses?" I asked.

"Well, to quote from the 'Appeals Section' of the *Personnel Policies Manual*, 'management is entitled to present whatever evidence is necessary to support its case.' This case will require the testimony of witnesses."

"Chet, why can't you just write it up in your paragraph, then we can have our meeting and it will be over with."

"Because it won't be over with. If we don't settle this right now, every staff support person who gets less than an excellent rating will file an appeal. My staff and I don't have time for that bullshit. So I want to make it perfectly clear that we do not underrate our support staff around here. If we do err, perhaps it's on the generous side."

"But, Chet, isn't calling in witnesses a bit of overkill?" I asked, attempting to appeal to some sense of his humanity. Unfortunately, I learned later that Chet only appeared human. His real origin is still unknown.

"I intend to prove through a preponderance of evidence that Dawn deserved no higher than a satisfactory rating."

"And you can't do that in a simple paragraph?"

"I told you—I intend to use Dawn as an example," Chet insisted.

"Do you think you could let me in on the plan? After all, I'm the one who's supposed to coordinate your efforts."

"Fine. I plan to call in everyone she has ever done work for and get their sworn testimony."

"Sworn testimony!" I laughed in astonishment. "Chet, this is an informal appeals hearing, not a courtroom trial. That's ridiculous. Dawn's a transcriber in the word processing pool. She's probably done work for thirty-five people over the past two years."

"Thirty-three to be exact."

I wasn't sure how this story was going to play out. My gut told me Chet was not about to hand me the condensed version.

"You can't be serious about bringing all those people into our personnel review meeting?" I asked him.

"Dead serious."

"But that could take all day."

"Precisely."

"So what's your point?"

"I've already told you. You just don't want to listen, my boy," he said in a condescending lawyer-like tone. "Dawn asked for this, didn't she? I'm just going to make sure she gets what she deserves," Chet said with a wicked smile.

I was helpless. There was nothing I could do to stop this train. I just had to hang on for the ride and try to keep my lunch steady. With that in mind I headed for my office to grab some *Mylanta*.

The following week Chet came to my office. "What type of budget do you have for witness transportation costs?"

"Witness transportation costs? We don't have any allocation for that. What are you talking about?"

"I'm going to need to fly in Hal Thornton from Chicago," he responded smugly.

"Chicago? Why do you need to fly in Hal Thornton? He's been gone six months."

"Dawn did some typing for Hal."

"Well, so what! She did typing for thirty-some others around here. Can't anyone here do?"

"Nope."

"Why not?" I was really feeling jerked around by this time.

"She did especially shitty work for Hal."

"And I suppose he has direct recall of each time she made a typo?"

"He's our star witness. He kept copies of all his drafts—from rough to complete. They tell a wonderful story."

"And he took these drafts with him to his new job in Chicago?"

"Hal's compulsive."

"And you say he needs to fly in to testify?"

"Yep."

"I give up—do what you need to do. I'll approve the expense out of the personnel budget." I conceded because I had no idea how to handle this. I was getting in deeper and deeper. He had strangled me with my own policy.

If I had known what I know today, I would have taken Dawn aside and told her and the union rep that the staff intended to filet her. The staff would use all available guerrilla tactics, and she would not only lose but also probably be destroyed in the process. The union rep would agree, we would convince her to drop it, and everybody would be happy. Unfortunately, I had no such advice to provide her. I still shudder when I think about what they did to her.

About a week before the hearing, I made a feeble attempt to modify the situation.

"Say, Chet, how does this sound? Why don't you just depose Hal over the telephone?"

"Can't."

"Why not?"

"He's only available on the date of the hearing. Besides, the agency has already bought his ticket—one of those nonrefundable deals."

"My tax dollars at work," I thought and walked back in my office and popped another *Mylanta.*

Dawn's hearing was scheduled for 9:00 A.M. Six other hearings were scheduled to follow hers that day. None of them made it. Chet and his evil gremlins planned to make a real party of it. Dawn had about as much chance of escaping this hearing unscathed as a paratrooper who's been dropped in shark-infested water during a feeding frenzy.

Two union representatives, a manager-at-large who was selected from a sister agency, Chet, twenty-seven other witnesses, and I all sat in the hearing room. The remaining five witnesses were on vacation, but Chet had their depositions at hand.

Chet first swore in Dawn and then proceeded to annihilate her testimony. Without a pause, he began to parade each witness up to the "stand." He swore them in and interrogated them about the quality of Dawn's work. The at-large manager was aghast as he watched the proceedings. He asked me if they could do this. I was embarrassed to tell him, "Yes." The union guys looked helpless. It was a nightmare.

To get the full impact of Chet's predatory action, here's an excerpt of the transcript that includes testimony from Dawn and another witness:

"State your full name, please."

"Dawn Marie Collins."

"Ms. Collins, how long have you worked for this agency?"

"Three years."

"And what type of employee do you consider yourself?"

"Hardworking and conscientious."

"Hardworking and conscientious. I see. Do you take breaks, Ms. Collins?"

"Yes, we're allowed to take scheduled breaks."

"And do you ever extend your breaks beyond the scheduled time?"

"No."

"Never, Ms. Collins? I just happen to have testimony from depositions taken from four attorneys. Each state that they have observed you extending your break by as much as

three minutes. I have the dates right here. Can you explain to this panel why you blatantly stole time from the government?"

"Well, I might have stayed a moment or two too long. I guess I may not have been watching the time closely."

"But these same attorneys have also testified that you do glance at your watch frequently. This has been observed particularly during the times just prior to lunch and quitting time."

"What does this have to do with my performance?"

"I'll tell you exactly what it has to do with your performance. Glancing at your watch while you're listening to dictation tapes has distracted you and caused you to make typos and punctuation errors."

"I hardly think that an occasional glance at my watch affects my work that drastically."

"Take a look at this, Ms. Collins. Do you recognize this document?"

"Yes, it's a legal brief."

"Let the record state that the witness has examined Exhibit A . . . . Now, Ms. Collins, you say this is a legal brief?"

"Yes."

"Any legal brief?"

"I don't know."

"You don't know? Aren't these initials on the bottom yours?"

"Well, yes, I suppose they are."

"Well, Ms. Collins, the computer log shows that this document was typed at 11:50 A.M. It also has ten identified errors circled by Hal Thornton. Would you say now, Ms. Collins, that looking at your watch near lunch time does not affect the quality of your work?"

I had to admire Dawn. She held up pretty well in spite of the grilling. However, things became increasingly macabre as the day wore on. As Chet marched in witness after witness, I was reminded of a game show where the host was yelling, "Come on down!" These folks spewed out testimony that disparaged and slashed Dawn's work with such joy, you'd think they were after the prize behind door number two.

"John, has Dawn Collins ever worked for you?"

"Yes."

"For how long?"

"About seven months."

"How would you assess the quality of her work?"

"Lame."

"Could you be more specific?"

"She makes errors on legal briefs."

"How about on your memos?"

"She makes errors on those too."

"Can you describe the nature of these errors?"

"Typos, misspelling, punctuation—the standard fare of incompetence."

"Do you feel that her performance rating of satisfactory is accurate?"

"Absolutely not."

"What do you feel would be a fair assessment?"

"Poor. She's terrible . . . I mean the worst. I'd fire her if I had the authority. I've started giving my stuff to Peggy as a matter of fact."

"Thank you. You may step down now. Panel, I'd like to call my next witness . . . ."

After the seventeenth witness had ripped the last vestiges of self-confidence from Dawn, she ran from the room with tears streaming down her cheeks.

Chet, still wired, was disappointed that his "trial" was aborted. I wouldn't be surprised if he was saving the best for last. Fortunately, we never had to find out. But he, with the help of his lynch mob, won "Viper of the Year." This mean, vicious courtroom drama was outright inhuman. One of the most frustrating parts was that I couldn't do a damn thing to Chet, and he knew it. I can somewhat understand his warped need to make a joke out of the agency's personnel policies. But what I'll never comprehend was his bona fide pleasure in doing it at the expense and destruction of another human being.

I found Dawn's resignation on my desk the next day.

 The personnel manager or his boss should have gone to Chet's boss. This situation could and should have been nipped in the bud. Even after the situation was over, Chet should have had to justify why he spent excessive government time and money.

What can I say? Lawyers are killers.

Legal Comments

A COBRA INCOGNITO

Gina started with the company as a college senior, working the six-to-nine evening shift in the telemarketing unit. She was a master on the telephone, earning commissions that covered tuition and a couple of new outfits each quarter. When she finished her degree, the company offered her a full-time job in a technical unit.

Gina was married to Dominic by then, but she began to find the relationship confining. He complained about her extended hours at the office. This annoyed her. She was having fun flirting with co-workers over drinks at the end of the day.

Gina had perfected the art of flirtation. She could use her sultry black eyes to flash a sexual message as clear and bright as a Forty-second Street neon. Since Gina had been an average student, she knew this was her only ticket to the fast track. With total precision, she selected targets to receive her carefully-crafted messages. Gina had the innate ability to know who wanted to dabble and who wanted to dip. She loved the attention, especially the following day as they lingered longingly at her desk.

"Dom is in the way. I can't breathe," she thought. "I'm twenty-three years old and just starting out on my career. Time to dump him. He's served his purpose."

Gina never told Dom about her promotion to corporate headquarters. One weekend she packed up her car, drove to Indianapolis, and found an apartment. She had instructed her attorney to handle everything without her. She returned to Providence when her court date was arranged and settled their divorce before they celebrated their second anniversary. She left immediately and grabbed the first plane home.

Gina ordered another cocktail and looked out the window of the plane. It was gray and overcast, but she felt full of sunshine. What could be better? She was doing very well on her job, and she had just unloaded her husband.

When she walked in the office that morning, she was faced with a surprise. A tall, attractive, blond woman was sitting at a desk smack next to hers. Gina hung up her coat and said hello.

"Hi, I'm Katherine Stewart," the woman responded and extended her hand, giving Gina a firm, confident grasp. "I've recently been assigned to your unit. I hope you don't mind the seating arrangements. They promised to get me my own cubicle soon."

Gina forced a return smile, introduced herself, and immediately headed for the ladies room where she could think. Her olive skin began to flush as something triggered an internal siren that howled and screeched a warning message throughout her head. Gina winced with pain as she heard the message repeatedly blare: "COMPETITION! . . . COMPETITION! . . . COMPETITION!"

"I need to get the scoop on her," Gina thought. "What's going on? Why didn't Bill tell me about this?" she worried. She concentrated on a spot on the wall to calm herself. "I'll just ask Bill and find out," she decided and walked to her boss's doorless office and tapped on the wall.

"Hi, Bill."

"Why, hello, Gina," Bill beamed. "Did you have a nice trip to Providence?"

"Very nice. I enjoyed seeing my folks. It was fun," she lied and noticed her hand was shaking slightly. "Tell me, who is this Katherine Stewart wedged next to my desk?" she asked.

"Oh, I'm sorry I didn't get a chance to fill you in, Gina, but I just found out myself. It's kind of a long and convoluted story."

"Well, fill me in," said Gina, masking her anxiety.

"Katherine worked for administrative services on a two-year contract. She had successfully completed her project, and the company wanted to hire her full-time. Unfortunately, there were no positions open in

Administrative Services, so Human Resources called our V.P. He knew one of our analysts was leaving in a few weeks and wanted to capitalize on grabbing up some hot talent. He made an executive decision and hired Katherine to replace the position even before our analyst left. Needless to say, there'll be some overlap for awhile," Bill explained. "I'm sorry you have to be inconvenienced with the tight seating arrangements."

"You mean she's going to work for you, and you didn't even get a chance to interview her and decide if you wanted her?" Gina asked incredulously.

"I was on vacation when the decision was made. It's no big deal, Gina, these things happen sometimes. Let's try to make the best of it."

"Well, can you tell me a little about her background?"

"Sure, she has a Ph.D. in marketing. She's primarily interested in corporate research and ultimately wants to work for Marketing, since her strength is in statistics and research. Even though this department is somewhat out of her area, she'll probably be with us for about a year before moving on. I'm sure she'll do fine."

"Is there anything you want me to do to help make her feel comfortable?" Gina asked, pitching her charm to insure her place as Bill's favored analyst.

"Just get her familiar with the branch offices and our procedures. That would be nice."

"Fine," Gina smiled and spun around to return to her desk feeling weak and nauseated. "Ph.D.—I can't have that," she thought. "I've been here three months and have established my position. She's not going to swoop in here and make me look like I'm a nobody. I've got to figure out a plan."

Katherine was a compulsive workaholic. She was not much for networking and led a fairly quiet life. She'd been married for several years and kept her distance from the men in the company. Although she did nothing to invoke their hostility, they tended to be intimidated by her.

Katherine was not very savvy about corporate politics. She asked difficult questions that sometimes put people on the spot. She didn't do these things with an intent to make others uncomfortable; she simply wanted to know the answers. It never occurred to her that these questions might make them feel foolish. Her academic grounding had always encouraged tough questions, and professors always praised her for her insightful queries. When Gina learned that Katherine was not well-liked by the men in the office, she decided to capitalize on this and plotted a multi-phased plan of destruction.

Phase I of Gina's plan was structured to destroy Katherine's credibility. Gina began by feeding Katherine misinformation about the personalities of branch office managers. Gina knew the branch managers had a collective need to have their "hinies" kissed at regular intervals. It didn't take her long to figure out that Katherine's no-nonsense style would be the perfect offender. So when Katherine asked Gina if any special procedures were necessary for informing Ralph Green at the Carbondale branch of their upcoming audit, Gina said, "Oh, just write him a memo and state when we've scheduled a review of their office. The branch handles all the other details."

"And by the way," Gina added, "mention that we need to have reports from the KSD-450 system prior to our arrival, so we can conduct a partial desk audit."

"Does any one else need to be copied?" Katherine asked.

"Oh, no," Gina assured her. "Bill counts on us to handle this on our own." Gina knew that if Bill were copied on the memo, he'd intercede as soon as he read it. So Ralph's irate call to Bill came as a complete surprise.

"Bill, who the hell is this Katherine Stewart you've got working in your department," Ralph shouted.

"She's our new analyst," Bill answered. "What seems to be the problem?"

"Well, I don't know what kind of high horse this broad is riding, but I'd like to know where she gets off telling me to schedule my time around your audit! I can't believe her nerve! And on top of that she asked us to have the KSD-450 reports ready. Doesn't she do her homework? We dropped that system eight months ago. What kind of flunkies are you hiring in your shop, Bill?"

Bill was astounded. He knew that Katherine was known to be a take-charge type, but he couldn't imagine that she would send a memo to the field without his knowledge. "Ralph, I regret you've had this trouble. I'll look into this and see if I can get the matter corrected."

When Bill called Katherine into his office to tell her about the problem, she grew silent. If she revealed that Gina had given her all this misinformation, she instinctively knew Gina would deny it. Gina's closeness to Bill was obvious, even to Katherine. Katherine was the new kid on the block, and she had to keep her mouth shut. Although she wasn't sure why, it was clear that Gina had set her up. She'd just have to be more careful next time.

"Bill, I guess I should have asked more questions before charging ahead on this. I'm sorry. I'll call Ralph and smooth things over," she said apologetically. "It won't happen again."

Katherine's call placated Ralph. Even though she was known to be very direct, she could deliver charm if she reached very deeply. Her credibility was at stake. She had no idea that in the months to come, her ultimate survival would depend on her wits and every other available resource.

Several weeks later, Bill called Gina and Katherine into his office. "I'm leaving the company," he announced.

"Leaving?" Gina's eyes widened.

"Yes, when they staffed Howard in the position above me, I decided to let myself be romanced by another company. I'll be leaving in two weeks."

Gina was upset. Although Gina never consummated her relationship with Bill—he was too straight-laced—her flattery sufficiently influenced him to give her plum assignments that offered the best exposure.

Katherine, on the other hand, was delighted with the news. She knew this turn of events would weaken a link in Gina's network of supporters. Katherine and Bill were scheduled to attend an industry meeting in St. Louis for three days. With Bill's departure planned a week before the meeting, Howard would have to accompany her instead. This would give Katherine the opportunity to gain an advantage over Gina.

Gina's mind clicked on furiously. She needed to somehow sabotage the upcoming industry meeting. After some careful thought, she put Phase II into action.

One evening Gina slyly waited around the office until only she and Howard remained. She stood outside his office and politely knocked on his partially opened door. "Howard, could I see you a moment?"

"Sure," he welcomed Gina. "Please sit down."

Howard was about ten years shy of retirement, but he looked older than his actual years. His white hair and conservative manner set a tone of honesty, loyalty, and company commitment. He was very uncomfortable about the upcoming trip with Katherine. He had never traveled with a woman before, and he was getting some static about it from his wife.

"I'm not sure how to begin this, Howard. I don't like to carry tales," Gina feigned flawlessly, "but I'm just concerned about your reputation."

"My reputation? Where could she possibly be headed?" he thought.

"What's troubling you?" he asked in a fatherly way, attempting to conceal his distress.

"Well, I know you've got a trip planned with Katherine. I just think you need to be careful. She confided in me that she thinks the men in this company are trying to stifle her career. She told me that she's planning a sex discrimination suit against the company. I'm just worried that she'll seize this trip as an opportunity to fuel her case. She may even try to build in some sexual harassment."

"Have you mentioned this to any one else, Gina?"

"No, of course not, Howard," she assured him.

"Fine. Let's keep it that way. I appreciate the input."

Gina could read by his expression that she had planted a very destructive seed. She just needed to water and fertilize it periodically, and Katherine's fate would be guaranteed. Gina felt very good about her plan.

When Katherine returned from her trip with Howard, she was upset and puzzled. Howard had seemed like a reasonable man. His actions during the trip were quite bizarre. He wouldn't meet her for breakfast or dinner and took off for a Cardinal's baseball game every evening. His lack of courtesy did not fit with his style.

Katherine suspected that Gina had her hand in this and called Gina at home that evening. "Gina, I've just got to tell you something. My trip with Howard was a disaster. The whole time we were together he treated me like a leper. He couldn't get away from me fast enough. Have you ever been treated so poorly on a business trip?"

"I can't speak for Howard," Gina said unemotionally. "I don't know him that well."

Her lack of surprise was a dead giveaway to Katherine. If Katherine would have had a videophone, she was sure that she'd see Gina rubbing her hands together with glee.

Gina had offended Katherine's sense of fair play for the last time. "This calls for the big guns," Katherine thought. "I hate like hell to use my brainpower for such a malevolent purpose, but the woman has left me no choice. She's dead meat."

Katherine then proceeded to forge a plan with the skill and passion of Michelangelo. She cleverly arranged to have Bill's position filled by Brent, a close personal associate whose integrity was beyond reproach. She warned him of Gina's sexual maneuvers and underhanded tactics. At this point, all Katherine had to do was sit back and observe Gina's fall from grace. Brent scrutinized Gina's work and found it lacking in substance. Gina began to crumble under the pressure to perform her job at his level of expectation. Once exposed, Gina fled the company without a shred of dignity and no job in sight.

Panel Comments Two wrongs don't make a right! We have all known some variation of this situation. It's sad to think that managers and fellow employees still make important decisions on feelings, not facts. Although Katherine also "gave what she got" in a more acceptable scenario, this feels like a very childish way to handle things and sets a bad pattern for the future. Although Gina's work may have lacked substance, the manager should have called upon Human Resources to help counsel and salvage Gina.

7
FLASHERS
AND
HARASSERS

It's probably easier to raise the consciousness of a sexual harasser than to lower the flag of a flasher. When threatened by the loss of a job, harassers learn very quickly that their sexual games of power and control are unacceptable. Unfortunately, fear of dismissal doesn't tend to deter flashers with equal effectiveness. Sadly, *they* are often the victims—powerless to control their urges. For them, extensive therapy may be a better alternative than unemployment.

FAIRY DUST

The print shop supervisor called the human resources manager about 7:15 that morning. "Celia, this is Robby Stewart. Please get down here. My offset operator just punched out one of our accountants, and the guy's flat on his back!"

"Is he conscious?" Celia asked immediately.

"No, out cold," Robby answered.

"Did you call 911 for the paramedics?" Celia worried.

"Yes, that was the first thing I did, but I thought you would want to be on the scene when they arrived. I also called our volunteer emergency team to help out in the interim. I see them coming right now."

"Good thinking, Robby. What's the accountant's name?"

"Malcolm Johnston."

"And the puncher?"

"Dwayne Ambrose."

"Thanks, I'll be right there," she said and gathered her note pad and purse.

"Phil," Celia said, "please pull Malcolm Johnston's and Dwayne Ambrose's files. Have them on my desk immediately. I have an emergency here." She flew out the door and down the three flights of stairs to the print shop.

Celia's mind raced. Nothing like this had ever happened. She'd heard of fights breaking out in manufacturing plants—but in an accounting firm? Nothing in her experience prepared her for what she was about to discover.

Celia arrived in the print shop just as the paramedics were wheeling Malcolm Johnston away on a gurney. He was conscious by this time and had an ice pack on his jaw. She asked to ride in the emergency vehicle with Malcolm, who lay on the gurney wincing. She held his hand and offered words of support. The hospital was less than five minutes away, and they were fortunate that this was

Monday morning. Mondays are usually quiet in an emergency room, so Malcolm was seen immediately. X-rays and other tests revealed that nothing was broken, and a concussion was not likely.

Celia asked Malcolm for his car keys, license number, make, and model. Then she gave Malcolm cab fare and told him to go home and rest. She promised to arrange for someone to return his car that evening and told him to report to her office first thing the next morning.

When she returned to her office, the puncher, Dwayne Ambrose was waiting in the reception room. "Hello, Dwayne, I'm Celia Cronen. I'll be with you in just a moment. Just let me get settled." She motioned to Phil to join her in her office. She briefed Phil on the details and asked him to notify Malcolm's supervisor about the incident. Phil left her office and she began to quickly review the files.

Malcolm was single and forty-four years old. He had been with the company for nearly ten years. His performance record was excellent, and he held a good reputation among his co-workers. He was also a part-time minister.

Dwayne had been with the company six years. He began in the mail room and worked his way to the print shop. He also had excellent performance records and had been a model employee. He was married and had a one-year-old child.

"Dwayne, please come in," Celia smiled.

Although it had been nearly an hour and half since the incident, tension remained on Dwayne's face. "Dwayne, would you like to tell me what happened?" she began.

"It all started when my car broke down."

"When your car broke down?" she repeated.

"Yes. There's a whole group of us who start work at 7:30. Well, we all meet for breakfast about 6:45 or 7:00. We talk about sports . . . tell jokes . . . whatever seems interesting, you know."

"Sure," Celia commented.

"Well, that's how I got to know Malcolm. He's been with our group for several years now. About three months ago, my wife and I were having car problems—one of our cars went on the blink—so we were trying to jockey our schedules to arrange transportation. I happened to mention this problem at breakfast one morning, and Malcolm offered to drive me home that evening."

"Did you accept?" Celia asked.

"Sure. I thought it was a nice gesture, and I appreciated it. Malcolm had always seemed like a good guy. With him being a minister and all, I never would have thought he was a pervert."

"A pervert?" Celia interjected.

"You know, gay."

"What makes you think he's gay?" she asked innocently.

"Well, he made a pass at me on the way home."

"A pass?" Celia wasn't quite sure how this was accomplished, so she asked, "Could you be more specific, Dwayne?"

"Well, he started talking about how attractive he thought I was, and then he asked me when I thought my wife was going to be getting home . . . and said how much he'd like to be with me."

Celia was beginning to get uncomfortable at this point, but she kept her composure.

"I was totally shocked and couldn't wait to get out of the car," Dwayne continued. "I told him I wasn't interested—I was a happily married man. No thanks."

"So that's why you knocked him out the next day," she offered, hoping this story was ready to end and spare her further exposure.

"No. No. Like I said earlier, that all happened several months ago. You see, he started sending me these love letters. He talked about his feelings for me and used terms I had never heard of like 'honey dipper' and 'golden shower' to describe his sexual feelings."

"What the hell is a *honey dipper* and a *golden shower?*"
Celia thought, but she was afraid to ask. So, instead she
inquired, "Were these letters typed or handwritten?"

"Handwritten."

"Do you still have them?"

"Hell, no, I tore them up. Who would want to save such
trash?! The man is sick. Sick, I tell you!"

"Did anyone else see these letters, like your wife, for
example?"

"No, I didn't want her exposed to this, but I did show
them to my buddy in the print shop."

"And who was that?

"Luther Taylor."

"Anyone else?" she asked, regaining her composure.

"No. Luther has known me for years, so he knew I
wouldn't encourage this. I didn't dare show anyone else."

"So, what specifically provoked you today?" she got up
her courage to ask.

"Well, when I didn't respond to his letters, he threatened
to put a voodoo curse on me. He called it something like
the curse of 'John de Cockatoo' or 'John de Conqueroo.' I
can't remember exactly."

"What was this 'John de whatever' curse supposed to
do?" she asked calmly, while silently humming the theme
song from *The Twilight Zone.*

"Malcolm said something about chanting the curse while
spreading some kind of fuji or wooji dust. I don't know. It
was all very weird. He claimed it would change my
feelings and get me to fall in love with him."

"Did he follow through with this curse?"

"Yes, unfortunately, yes," Dwayne said.

Celia could see that Dwayne was becoming agitated
again. "How do you know?" she asked, somewhat afraid to
hear the response.

"Because someone broke into my apartment and
spread this strange stuff all over my living room floor. I

didn't notice it at first. All I noticed was that a window was broken. Nothing was missing. I made a police report about the break-in, but nothing was missing so they didn't dust for prints. They just looked at the window, took the report, and left in a half hour. Later that evening, when my wife came home with the baby and the baby was crawling around the living room floor, he started coughing and wheezing. That's when I noticed it."

"Noticed what?" she asked.

"I saw strange powdery stuff scattered on the floor. We wound up having to take the baby to the hospital last night. The doctor said he must have had an allergic reaction."

"Is the baby okay now?" Celia asked with genuine concern.

"He's fine, no thanks to Malcolm," Dwayne's voice began to rise. "Then this morning Malcolm comes up to me with this stupid look of self-satisfaction on his face and snickered, 'How do you feel about me today?'"

"So, I said, 'I won't tell you how I feel, I'll show you how I feel,' and I let him have it. It happened very fast."

"I see," was all Celia could say. She was so stunned by this story that she was trying to gather her thoughts for the next question. Then she cleared her throat and added, "Do you have a copy of the emergency room report?"

"Sure, I have it with me because I was going to submit it to benefits."

"I'd like to make a copy of it. In the meantime, I'd like you to take the next two days off until I can complete my investigation. Report to work as usual on Wednesday."

"Will I get paid for these days, or am I suspended without pay?" Dwayne asked with grave concern.

"I don't know yet," Celia responded. "It will depend on the outcome of the investigation."

Dwayne left the office, and Celia immediately called his supervisor.

"Hi, Robby, this is Celia. Malcolm is okay, he's home resting, and I've sent Dwayne home for a couple of days to cool off. I need to see Luther Taylor immediately. Can you send him up?"

"Sure, what's going on?" Robby asked.

"I'll fill you in when the investigation is complete," she assured him.

Celia interviewed Luther who confirmed having seen the letters. Neither he nor anyone else in the area overheard the verbal interchange between Dwayne and Malcolm prior to the incident. No one actually saw Dwayne deliver the punch to Malcolm. The next day, Celia interviewed Malcolm. He denied everything. Based on the evidence, Celia decided to treat this as a sexual harassment case. Neither party received any reduction in pay for their temporary suspension, but Celia instructed Malcolm that he was to have no further contact with Dwayne again. She worked with their respective supervisors to rearrange lunch hours so future opportunity for contact would be limited. The harassment ceased, but shortly thereafter Malcolm quit and took a job with another company.

 Celia did a reasonably thorough job on this case
Panel and covered most of the angles—witnesses,
Comments reports, emergency response, suspensions, etc. However, Malcolm needs help and should have been given the option of counseling. Many companies provide paid confidential counseling if made through formal supervisory referral. Also, Celia should make it clear to Dwayne that violence is not taken lightly, even if provoked.

This was correctly perceived as a sexual harassment case, even though it does not fit into
Legal Comments the more commonplace male manager/female

subordinate model. As a rule of thumb, an employer can be liable for the harassing acts of a nonsupervisor if the employer knew or should have known of the offensive conduct.

The personnel manager's instinct to conduct an investigation was correct. Indeed, the key to success in sexual harassment situations is to promptly investigate, document the investigation, and take prompt, appropriate, corrective action. One subtle pitfall to be wary of: the victim must not be inadvertently penalized as part of the solution. For example, transferring a victim of sexual harassment to a department or shift that is viewed as less desirable may be a satisfactory solution from the company's perspective, but the victim may believe he or she was retaliated against for complaining. This would be unlawful.

SUPPLEMENTAL PAY

Sherilyn walked into Walter's office with a bright and sunny smile. "Hi, Walt, how're ya doin'?"

"Wonderful, Sherilyn. Are you feeling better this week?"

"Oh, much better, thank you. That flu was a killer!" she remarked. "By the way, Walter, could I please have my paycheck? It was issued the week I was out."

"I'm sorry, Sherilyn, no can do," he smiled innocently.

Sherilyn was startled. "What do you mean?"

"Well, there's this new policy now. It states that you have to be present the day before and the day after paychecks are due to receive one."

"Come on, Walter, when did this *new* policy go into effect?" she questioned him sarcastically.

"Oh, it's always been available to supervisors," he informed her. "It's one that can be invoked under supervisory discretion, and I decided that you're not eligible for your paycheck," he said with all seriousness.

"Look, Walt, I've had about enough of this nonsense," she said, attempting to control her fury. "Just who do I have to see to get my paycheck if it isn't you?"

The look on Walter's face took on a lecherous pose, and he responded to her question by opening his middle desk drawer and placing two crisp hundred dollar bills on his desk. "Listen, Sherilyn, you'll get this *and* your paycheck if you meet me at the Alabaster Inn this evening. I promise you a very exciting night."

"How dare you, Walter! You disgust me! Give me my paycheck, and give it to me now," she demanded.

"No," Walter insisted.

Seething, Sherilyn stormed out of his office and sailed across the hall and past the president's secretary's desk so fast that she sent all loose items airborne. She barged into his office and demanded an audience.

The president had known Sherilyn for four years. He had never seen her in this state and couldn't imagine what was wrong.

"Calm down, Sherilyn, what is it?"

"Calm down! Calm down! You calm down!" she shrieked. "That repulsive reptile, Walter, just told me that I needed to sleep with him in order to get my paycheck. He even had the gall to wave hundred dollar bills in my face as some sort of enticement. Then he said he was invoking some insane policy about not getting my paycheck because I wasn't here the day before and the day after it was issued. I should have maced that bastard. My mace is in my purse." Then her eyes darted about the room. "Where's my purse. Where is it?" She was becoming hysterical at this point.

No one had ever reacted to Walter's games so violently before. The president wasn't quite sure how to handle this one.

The president had Sherilyn's check in his hand. "Sherilyn, please sit down."

"I don't want to sit down; I just want my paycheck," she insisted.

"Of course you'll get your paycheck. Walter was just pulling a practical joke on you. Here's your check. I'll talk to him. I'm sure he won't do it again."

Sherilyn snatched her check and stomped off. The president called Walter. "Walter, I thought we discussed this once before about three years ago. You're to stop that paycheck nonsense. Do you hear me?"

"Sure, Jack. I won't do it again. You know I was just funnin'."

"I know, Walter, but today's women don't find it funny, so please stop it. One of these days, you're going to get yourself hurt. Sherilyn was ready to come in and mace you! In her state, I wouldn't have been surprised if she kicked you once you were down."

"Okay, okay. Nobody seems to have a sense of humor any more," Walt muttered to himself, not understanding why Sherilyn had created such a brouhaha. "What's wrong with these women? They just can't take a joke, just can't take a joke," he lamented as he picked up his hundred dollar bills and folded them neatly into his wallet.

Panel Comments The company should have thwarted Walter's "little games" long ago. The president's awareness and inaction over this and Walter's prior offenses not only places the company at risk but also fosters an untenable situation for employees assigned to Walter. It's clear that Walter doesn't understand the gravity of the situation. Letting him off the hook this time was a serious mistake.

Legal Comments Two principal issues arise here. First, if Sherilyn had left the premises rather than go to the president's office, the company and/or Walter may have faced criminal liability. Under many state labor laws, refusal to tender paychecks is not only unlawful but also a misdemeanor.

Second, this employer will be truly lucky if no sexual harassment suit is filed. When an employee complains about sexual harassment, it is vital that the company respond appropriately. This may be the last opportunity the employer has to resolve the matter without formal proceedings. It should always be the company's goal to try to resolve these situations without forcing the victim to seek the intercession of an outside party (e.g., private attorney, state agency, union).

This particular company is truly on thin ice because the president evidently knew of Walter's proclivities from prior episodes and failed to take prompt, appropriate, corrective action when Sherilyn complained to him. Unless this company implements a sexual harassment policy promptly, including training of supervisory personnel such as Walter, it will remain a ticking time bomb for a litigation explosion.

OVEREXPOSED

Alexandra had run an errand outside the building. On her way back to her office; she was the only one to enter the elevator at the lower-lobby level. When she pressed the button for the fifteenth floor, the doors closed, and she stepped to the rear of the elevator. After the elevator advanced to the fourth floor, it stopped automatically. A tall, average-looking man entered and greeted her with a friendly smile, which she courteously returned. He pressed the nineteenth floor, the doors closed, and the elevator proceeded to advance.

Then, without warning, the man whirled around, opened up his suit jacket exposing a full erection, and said lecherously, "How'd you like to have this?" Fortunately, within moments, the elevator stopped at Alexandra's floor, and she ran off.

Bewildered and shaking, Alexandra called Cal Jones in Human Resources. "Ca . . . Cal, this is Alexandra Flowers, Georgia Lawton's assistant. I have a problem. Can you come up immediately?"

"What's wrong?"

"I've just been flashed, and I'm too scared to get back on the elevator."

"I'll be right up," Cal assured her.

This was the third complaint that Cal had received in two weeks. Cal interviewed Alexandra to gather the facts. Her story was nearly identical to the other two complaints.

Cal knew the perpetrator had to be an employee. In all three instances, the man either entered or exited to the fourth floor, a floor not open to the public. But no one seemed to know who he was.

The company occupied twenty floors of the building. Each floor housed about one hundred fifty people. After gathering information from Alexandra, Cal asked her if she would be willing to tour the fourth floor and make a positive identification. Alexandra had regained her composure after talking with Cal, and her initial fright turned to outrage.

"Sure, let's find the sicko!" she said enthusiastically.

The two of them toured the fourth floor about one hour after the incident. Alexandra spotted the flasher immediately. Cal thanked her for her help and then called on Rosa and Lynn. He took each of them to the fourth floor on separate occasions. Each positively identified the same man that Alexandra had fingered.

Cal decided to do some further checking. The employee's name was Harley Meisterman. He had only been with the company six months. Cal called Harley's former employer in a city about seven hundred miles away and learned that Harley was terminated for indecent exposure. Cal decided to dig deeper. A closer check revealed that Harley had an arrest record for exposing himself in a department store on Christmas Eve the preceding year as well as a parole violation on a prior conviction for the same offense.

Cal put together the file of the Christmas Eve arrest, the parole violation report, the former employer's termination information, and the three recent employee complaints. Then he called Harley into his office.

"Harley, I have on my desk before me your arrest records and other employee complaints for indecent exposure. Which would you rather do, be prosecuted by the women involved or resign?"

Harley resigned. However, Harley had recently married a woman who worked for the company. She was a naive woman who had spent eight years in a convent before joining the company. When she learned of her husband's resignation, she stormed into Cal's office.

"I'd like to know why this company railroaded my husband into a resignation? This company has a reputation in the community for being a good place to work and treating its employees fairly. Well, I don't see how that can be when you do these kinds of things to your employees."

It was clear to Cal that Harley had not told her the reason for his resignation. So when Cal pulled out the file, he said, "Ellen, you've been married to Harley for nearly a year now. It's time that you knew something more about your husband. We didn't railroad him out of a job. Here's a copy of the newspaper account saying he was arrested on Christmas Eve. Read it." Then he handed her the parole violation report and employee complaints to review.

Instead of being shocked, Ellen's face looked as though a light bulb had been turned on. "Gee, maybe this explains why he does some of the things he does," she muttered.

"What do you mean?" Cal asked.

"Well, for one, he keeps ladies' underwear in the dresser drawer in his bedroom," she disclosed.

"*His* bedroom?" Cal slipped.

"Yes, he brings boyfriends home and they sleep in bed with him, and I sleep on the sofa. I was a little concerned at first. He said they were old drinking buddies. I just thought he hadn't weaned himself from them since we had only recently gotten married, and I figured it would clear itself up," she responded ingenuously.

It was Cal who was shocked now. It was hard for him to believe anyone in today's society could be so naive. Eventually, however, Ellen wised up and kicked Harley out. Cal was delighted when he was summoned to testify about Harley's activities at her annulment proceedings.

Panel Comments Cal should have encouraged the women to prosecute Harley. That would have given Ellen important information and perhaps would have been the blow needed to get Harley to seek help. All forms of sexual harrassment should be vigorously addressed by company officials.

Why did Cal wait until after Harley was hired to do some checking on Harley's background? **Legal Comments** Employers are increasingly being held liable for the conduct of their employees if the company was "negligent" in its selection process. Checking references and at least inquiring about prior criminal convictions are the bare minimum steps employers should take to reduce their risk of liability for "negligent hiring."

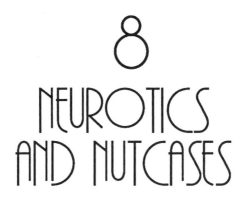

8
NEUROTICS
AND NUTCASES

Strange rangers can roam the floors of any company. Their weirdness may offer co-workers an enjoyable break from the monotony of day-to-day activity. Other times these characters can be outright unsettling. Their behavior comes in all forms, varying from simple cases of peculiar and annoying personal habits to frightening and destructive acts. Even with careful screening techniques, a few pass through the doors and are not discovered until they are on the job. Often, the culmination of daily stresses erodes their ability to cope as normal folks. For some of these time bombs, just one incident may set them off. It's scary to think you might be working right next to them.

THE HANDWRITING IS ON THE WALL

Jane and her friend Tracy met at their favorite cafe. Soft shell crabs were in season. As she tested them with her fork, Jane grinned. "This is great—having the best food with my best friend. Gosh, Tracy, there's so much gossip to catch up on, I don't know where to begin."

Tracy nodded in agreement and encouraged her. Before Jane knew it, the hour had vanished. She had covered the entire department and the one on the floor below. The friends laughed and giggled the whole time.

"Oh, waiter, could I have a refill on the lemonade, please?" Jane politely motioned. She checked her watch. "Whoops! I better get going. I don't want to be too late getting back."

Tracy hugged her good-bye and Jane raced her car up the highway. She ate too much. The food was wonderful, but she could have eaten half the amount. Her stomach was gurgling and swishing from all the lemonade. The speed bumps in the parking lot didn't make her any more comfortable.

She checked her watch again. She was two minutes late. "Need to make a quick pass through the restroom, " she thought. "Otherwise, I won't make it to my desk."

Her full bladder was sending signals of urgency. When she swung open the ladies' room door, she staggered. The smell was so vile that it stung her eyes and burned her nostrils. "PEE-UUU! It smells like a baby filled its diaper in here," she blurted aloud, screwing up her face and dashing to the nearest stall.

She struggled to get her pantyhose down and didn't even bother with seat paper. "God, I'm glad no one's in here. First there's this awful smell, and now I sound like a cow pissing on a flat rock," she thought. "Thank goodness everyone else is back from lunch."

Jane quickly washed her hands, whipped out a towel as fast as a frog snatches a dragonfly, and started out the door, when. . .

"YIIEECHHHHH!" she gagged.

She raced back to the sink and turned the water to Niagara strength. She turned her head away in disgust as she blasted the brown pasty foreign substance that she just collected from the push plate of the swinging door.

Then it happened. The lemonade that had settled so comfortably in her stomach decided to make a U-turn. The jolt sent Jane speeding toward the stall. Before she could raise the lid, she said good-bye to her lunch.

Jane felt like she was going to lose consciousness. Simultaneously chilled and perspiring, she managed to drag herself back to the sink and wipe her mouth and face. She had to get out of there.

This time Jane took some extra towels for protection and decided to brave the trip. The back of the door was smeared with excrement, and Jane faced the message for the second time. Scrawled in six-inch letters, "THE DEVIL IS MY SAVIOR" stared back at her.

She wrapped her fingers in the towels, held her breath, and closed her eyes. Then summoning up what strength she had left, she poked open the door with her gloved index and third fingers. Once through, she dropped the towels and sped down the hall, gasping for breath.

Still horrified and shaking, Jane ran to the Personnel Department. Pushing her way past the smiling, mannequin-like receptionist, she burst into the personnel manager's office and collapsed in a chair. Her head flopped to the side as she tried to regulate her breath.

By the terrified look in Jane's eyes and her heavy breathing, Gary instantly knew he had a severe problem. "What's wrong? Has someone tried to hurt you?"

"I . . . I . . . uh . . . I . . . um," Jane stammered. "The ladies' restroom . . . ." She fell silent.

"On this floor?" Gary asked.

Jane weakly nodded, "Yes."

"Suzanne, call security to investigate the ladies' restroom immediately," Gary shouted to his secretary.

"Can you tell me your name?" he asked quietly.

"J . . . Ja . . . Jane Montrose."

"Jane, did someone try to hurt you in the restroom?"

Jane looked at the floor and shook her head, "No."

Within a few minutes Brian Rath, the Corporate Security officer, stepped in the doorway of Gary's office. Brian was a big man, with hairy arms that bulged from his uniform. He was a retired narcotics detective and had started a second career with the company. He was good at his job. Brian had investigated and nabbed a couple embezzlers, cleaned up a minor drug problem, and kept the street people out of the lobby. He motioned to Gary. "Can I see you for a minute?"

Gary stepped out of the office, and Brian pulled him around the corner. "Christ, Gary, some pervert has taken shit and smeared it all over the door in the ladies' restroom. There's some kind of devil mumbo jumbo written too. I sent one of my boys to take a picture, and then the cleaning crew will get in there and sanitize it."

Gary was stunned. He had all kinds of experience with employee problems, but this one was too sick for him to think about.

"What are we going to do?" he asked Brian.

"Well, first of all, we don't know if this is an isolated incident or if it will happen again. We also don't know if it was done by an outsider or one of our employees. I suggest we keep it quiet and use some surveillance. I'll arrange to get things set up within a couple days."

Gary felt uneasy. Brian usually made him feel calm, but today was different. Gary walked back into his office to deal with Jane.

"Jane, I'm sorry you had to have such a dreadful experience. The cleaning crew is sanitizing the bathroom now, and our security force will be conducting an investigation. Now, I'm going to need your help. I think that it would be best if we didn't say anything to anyone at this time. Do you think you feel well enough to go back to your desk, or would you like to go home this afternoon?"

"I guess I'm okay, but what am I going to tell my boss? I'm nearly forty-five minutes late from lunch."

"I'll handle that," Gary assured her and winked. "Who is your supervisor?"

"Win Martinez."

Gary flipped through his interoffice directory and located Martinez. Using his speaker phone, he punched in the extension and waited for Martinez to answer.

"Win, Gary Holden here. Say, Win, I have one of your employees, Jane Montrose, in our Medical Department. Apparently she had an upset stomach after lunch and asked to lie down for awhile. She seems to be fine now. I'll be sending her up."

"Are you sure she doesn't need to go home?"

"No, she's fine."

"No problem then. I'm glad she's okay. Thanks, Gary."

"Bye," Gary said and disengaged his speaker phone.

"There, Jane, you heard it all. Everything is fine." Gary walked Jane out to the main office. Although he could feel his face muscles operating in the smile mode, Gary had a terrible feeling this was not going to be a simple case.

About a month later Midge Fontana, whose office was in the Risk Management Department on the third floor, arrived in Personnel. The receptionist, busily pasting address labels, was interrupted with the sensation of a menacing energy force. When she looked up, there was Midge, red-faced and nearly snorting.

Programmed to speak in cool personnel tones, the receptionist acknowledged Midge with the standard, "May I help you?"

"Where's Gary?"

"Mr. Holden is in a meeting now," she reacted automatically. "Did you have an appointment? I don't seem to see anyone listed after his 2:30," she added somewhat snidely.

"No, I don't have an appointment," Midge barked. "This is an emergency. Tell him I need to see him now!"

"One moment, I'll see if he can be interrupted," she responded mechanically and lifted the phone off her receiver. "Oh, could you tell me your name, please?"

"MIDGE FONTANA, DIRECTOR OF RISK MANAGEMENT!" Midge was rapidly losing patience with this ditz-brain.

The receptionist punched in Gary's number. "Mr. Holden, there's a Ms. Fontana here who would like to see you. She says it's an emergency."

Gary was baffled. Midge was one of the most respected managers in the company. Her reputation was built on her ability to stay cool in a tough situation. Gary's mind raced, "Midge's style would be to call me, not show up at my office. What could possibly be wrong?"

Gary excused himself from the interview he was conducting and stepped into the main lobby to greet Midge. Her teeth were clenched and both hands were formed into tight fists. "Midge, let's see if I can find an empty office." Gary put his arm around Midge's shoulder and guided her stiffened body away from the lobby.

Once behind closed doors, Midge exploded. "Gary, some disgusting slime has smeared shit all over the women's bathroom! It's revolting! I put an out-of-order sign up there so no one else would use it. What the hell is going on around here?"

"Midge, which floor was this restroom on?" he asked her.

"My floor, the third floor."

"The third floor?" he repeated raising his eyebrow.

"Yes, the third floor," she said again.

"Was there anything written?" Gary asked

"Frankly, I didn't stick around to find out. As soon as the smell hit me, I turned to the right and spotted a brown blob on the wall, so I got the hell out of there," Midge snarled.

"So you didn't notice if there was any writing?" Gary persisted.

"Look, Gary, I told you I was only in there a second. I suppose if I had seen writing, you'd want to know if the creep had good penmanship!" she quipped sarcastically.

"Look, Midge, I'm sorry if my questions seem strange. Please sit down. I'm calling Brian. We've got a real problem here."

Gary tapped out Brian's extension. "Brian, we've had another episode."

"Same restroom?"

"No, this time on the third floor. Midge Fontana discovered it. She posted an out-of-order sign on the door. Can you get someone to take pictures and then get the cleaning crew down there? We have to move quickly on this now, Brian. We'll have to beef up surveillance. It's got to be one of our employees. Outsiders don't have access to the third floor."

"I agree," said Brian and hung up.

Gary filled Midge in on the prior incident. Brian arrived shortly.

"Okay, Brian, what's your plan?"

"Well, security cameras are out, unless we want to set ourselves up for a whopping lawsuit," he joked.

Midge rolled her eyes in disapproval.

"Okay, then, what's our alternative?" interjected Gary.

"Well, I suggest we set up constant surveillance at each ladies' restroom. We can't use outside people, or the perpetrator could be scared away. I feel pretty sure this is an employee. We've got to find trusted employees we can put on special duty, some who can be spared from their regular stations. We've got three ladies' restrooms. We can set up two-hour shifts. To cover an eight-hour day, we need four women per john," Brian calculated. "That means we'll need a twelve-woman team. They'll be briefed on the stakeout activities. Basically, I'll have them observe the restroom from a distance, and each time someone enters and exits, they'll check out the conditions."

"How long do you think this will take?" Midge asked.

"It's hard to tell. We've had nearly a month between incidents. Something must trigger them," Brian responded.

The employees selected for the stake-out team were excellent. They were carefully briefed and never leaked a word. To establish a team identity, they privately referred to themselves as the C.R.A.P. squad—Coalition of Recruits Against Perversion.

After nearly six weeks of dogged surveillance, Charlotte Wilmer, assigned to the 1:00 - 3:00 P.M. shift, spotted Jenny Rentzer enter the third floor restroom at 2:17 P.M. and remain there until 2:32 P.M. No one else entered the facility. When Charlotte inspected, she found Jenny's message. This time it contained only expletives. Charlotte immediately posted an out-of-order sign and summoned Brian as per instructions. Brian arrived on the crime scene with his security crew. They dusted for finger prints, took pictures, and collected samples.

After the evidence was analyzed, Brian and Gary presented Jenny with the file. Jenny woefully admitted to the other incidents and explained that her life was disintegrating. In checking with Jenny's supervisor, they learned that Jenny's performance had also declined.

With Jenny's permission, the company arranged psychiatric counseling. Privacy laws assured that Jenny's psychiatric diagnosis and treatment would be kept confidential, just like any other medical records. No one but Jenny and her psychiatrist were privy to the real cause that motivated her behavior. Sadly, Jenny was never able to sufficiently recover to return to work, and she was eventually terminated.

Panel Comments The personnel manager earned his money on this one! Although this is a tragic case, the company protected the employee and managed to keep everyone else calm throughout the investigation. We commend all the individuals involved for insuring a business-as-usual environment during a very tense situation.

Legal Comments If the unfortunate Ms. Rentzer were able to return to work after therapy, her psychiatric disability (or her record of such disability) would probably not be sufficient basis to deny her continued employment—assuming she was otherwise qualified to perform the job.

Would she have a case for religious discrimination? ("The Devil is my Savior.") Pretty far fetched. Courts are reluctant to recognize religious beliefs not based on some recognized, bona fide religion or religious belief. For example, at least one court has rejected a religious discrimination claim based on the employee's claim that smoking marijuana was part of his religious liturgy. In this case, it is almost inconceivable that smearing excrement on bathroom walls would be viewed as the exercise of some genuine religious practice.

PANIC IN THE PARKING LOT

The company was committed to elevating its corporate conscience. Its aggressive campaign to search out and hire physically and mentally handicapped employees had earned national recognition as a model for all companies. Access ramps and electronic doors were common place. High-tech equipment, designed to assist physically and mentally impaired employees hummed busily throughout the facility. The research funds that the corporation poured into joint efforts with computer companies and universities had finally paid off. The flood of media attention made the organization the darling of the industry and the community. All of this was good for business.

Morton Highland was the company's respected general manager. His favorite activity was to host executives from other companies in their tour of the facility. He proudly explained the newest equipment and always delighted in introducing their "special" employees to the visitors. The last stop on the tour was usually his office. It was crowded with plaques and accommodations from various agencies and organizations. Each award spoke of the company's untiring commitment and applauded its efforts toward mainstreaming the mentally and physically challenged.

Alfred Manchester, who was mildly mentally handicapped, was one of the companies newest "special" employees. The company's industrial psychologist had assessed Alfred with interviews and a series of tests. The psychologist determined that the young, cherub-faced boy was capable of highly routine clerical or manual work. Alfred functioned best in a structured routine, so he was assigned to the print shop. There he bound reports, ran simple copy equipment, and maintained department logs.

The psychologist was on target. Alfred loved his job. He was always prompt, never wasted time, and was careful about his work. His supervisor often remarked that she wished she could have five Alfreds. When Alfred heard her make these comments, he extended his grin wider than usual, flashed an adoring look her way, and returned to work even more intently.

Alfred felt very lucky indeed. He found the smell of the inks and binding glue comforting. This was his first real job. He was on his own. Today he especially enjoyed the bright airy atrium where he chewed thoughtfully on the leftover roast beef sandwich his mom had packed for him.

"Everyone is so nice here, not like at school where the other kids teased and made fun of me," he thought as he rummaged through his lunch bag to see what kind of treat his mother had sent along this time. Alfred had been on the job for two months now, and everything was going along smoothly.

Alfred had never taken city busses before this job. At first, he was very nervous about taking the bus. Alfred had no problem counting change, because he and his mom always made sure he had the exact amount before he walked out in the morning. Just to be safe, he kept his bus fare in a separate section of his wallet. But the schedules were sometimes confusing. The office was in the suburbs, and the bus only ran every forty minutes. The thought of missing his bus made Alfred feel clammy and disoriented.

About a week later, Alfred's supervisor asked him to stay a few extra minutes so they could complete a rush project. Always eager to please, Alfred plunged into the task. This extra duty delayed Alfred by about fifteen minutes—just long enough to miss his bus. When he left the rear entrance of the building at 5:15 P.M., he looked for the familiar faces that rode the bus with him. No one was in sight.

A wave of nausea converged on Alfred. He felt himself starting to perspire. On the pavement, peeking through the melting snow, were chunks of asphalt coughed up from last winter's series of freezing and thawing. Alfred's eyes started to water while he grew more and more agitated. Frustrated, he grabbed a fistful of asphalt. It was now 5:30, and no bus was in sight.

Morton Highland decided to call it quits for the day. He packed up his briefcase and headed for the rear entrance, where his car was parked. As he walked through the door, a whirring sound and a shotgun snap cracked right past his ear. When he rubbed his ear, his fingers touched his cheek. He felt sand and grit.

Before Morton had a chance to look around, he felt a punch in his arm. Morton dropped his briefcase from the impact and spotted Alfred winding up to hurl another chunk of asphalt. Morton quickly grabbed his briefcase, shielding himself from Alfred's machine-gun like pellets as he ducked back in the building for safety. He raced to the nearest office to call for help.

A few minutes later, three sales managers walked down the hall. They were engrossed in swapping stories as they walked out the same rear door.

Alfred fired one torpedo and then another.

"Ow," yelped George, as he rubbed his thigh.

"Ouch," howled Rueben, grabbing his shoulder.

Jack, who hadn't completely walked out, observed the fracas and spied Alfred's glazed eyes and a handful of asphalt.

"Get in here, you guys," he motioned. "That's Alfred, he must have gone berserk or something."

All three scattered. Like cockroaches after a *Black Flag* blitz, they fled to safe crevices of the building. There they found Morton, hanging up the phone. By the look on their faces, Morton knew what had happened.

"You must have run into Alfred," Morton said.

"What are we going to do?" quivered George, still rubbing his thigh.

"Well, I certainly don't want to call the police. It will be bad for public relations," Mort maintained.

"But he's holding us hostage. I've got to get home for my daughter's recital. My wife will kill me if I'm late," Rueben whined as he massaged his throbbing shoulder.

"Look, I'm sure we can figure a way out of this, if we all put our heads together," Jack remarked casually. "Besides, how dangerous can he be? I mean . . . really!"

"Oh, that's easy for you to say. You didn't get hit by the flying shrapnel," Rueben argued.

"You're such a goddamn wimp, Rueben. If it's not your wife who's giving you the runs, it's a print-shop flunky. You'd think Alfred was touting an uzi, the way you're shaking. Look at yourself; you're white as a sheet."

Rueben's embarrassment drained all his energy. He silently slid down in a chair and stared stupidly out the window.

"Calm down, you guys," interrupted Morton. "I've asked Personnel to call his mom. She'll come and pick him up. He's just scared."

"Well, what are we supposed to do until she gets here?" Rueben asked, somewhat regaining his composure.

"Sit and wait," Morton replied matter-of-factly.

"Look, I told you I can't sit. I have to go to my daughter's recital," Rueben insisted.

"Well, if you want to brave it, take a garbage can lid from the lunchroom, and use it as a shield until you get to your car. Then lock yourself in and drive out in the opposite direction," Morton suggested.

"You guys won't feel like I'm abandoning you, will you?" Rueben squeaked. "I mean, you know how it is with kids."

"Fine, Rueben, go ahead. We'll try to cover for you while you make an ass of . . . er . . . I mean a dash for it," Jack promised, turning a contemptuous smirk toward Morton.

"Gee, guys, I really appreciate it," Rueben sang as he dashed off to the cafeteria for his guardian shield.

Covering his vitals with the protection of an industrial version of a Sears *Roughneck*, Rueben made it to his car, with only a slight bruise to his right calf. The rest of the managers remained in the building until Alfred's mom battled the traffic for a 7:00 P.M. arrival.

Unfortunately, the story does not end here. Alfred missed his bus on several other occasions. Each time Alfred panicked, which tested the conscience and patience of the company's management. The company, along with Alfred's mom, decided it was in Alfred's best interest to find a job that was closer to home, one in which his routine would not be upset.

Panel Comments There would appear to be some additional action that could have been taken by Alfred's supervisor and the personnel office. Certainly after the first incident, someone could have walked Alfred to the bus stop and helped him to get another bus. Given that Alfred could function in the workplace, some cooperative effort between his mother and the company might have salvaged a dedicated worker. Buses run on a schedule. It is highly unlikely that Alfred was working alone and unsupervised. The supervisor could have kept a schedule. With a little effort and compassion, there might have been a different ending.

Legal Comments This story highlights a likely problem for employers in the near future. Given the improvements in prenatal care and in emergency lifesaving birth procedures, the percentage of children who survive difficult births has dramatically increased. Unfortunately, many of these children are brain damaged or otherwise disabled. The resultant increase in our disabled population, coupled with the increased sensitivity to disabled persons and the recently enacted legal protections for the handicapped, suggests that discrimination on the basis of disability may well be the key EEO issue of the '90s and beyond.

While employers may not discriminate against otherwise qualified applicants on the basis of disability, they also have the right to deny employment to persons who are unable to do the job. In Alfred's case, the company would have to reasonably accommodate his handicap before discharging him. For example, a work schedule modification is a typical form of accommodation and might well have worked here so that Alfred would not miss his bus.

Unfortunately, once Alfred demonstrated a propensity for violence, the company would be well-advised to consider whether he should be retained as an employee. Any employee or passerby injured by Alfred in one of his frenzies would have a strong claim against the employer.

A PROBLEM OF EPIDEMIC PROPORTION

Bertha worked for a large computer software design corporation. Her job involved performing highly sophisticated computer programming activities. Unlike the application programmers who dealt with the nuts and bolts, Bertha was a member of an elite society. Considered the crème de la crème, she was the one who made the real magic. She solved the tough problems and kept the customers coming back. Unfortunately, Bertha's interpersonal skills were severely deficient. Consequently, the company never let the customer get a look at Bertha, who had a tendency to curl her lip when she growled. Her "trainer" kept Bertha behind the scenes to do her tricks. He always acted as liaison with the customer.

Bertha's less technical colleagues affectionately referred to her as a "bare metal" hacker. They joked among themselves that she and her terminal would be quite content locked in a closet with raw meat thrown in on occasion. They were unaware of Bertha's sensitive nature, especially her deep concern for the health and welfare of the community. No one would have had a clue if Bertha hadn't written a memo to Administrative Services one day. Actually, no one knew Bertha could communicate much beyond a grunt or a snarl.

TO: *Hollister Adams, V.P.*   DATE: *March 1, 1991*
      Administrative Services

FROM: *Bertha Weiler*   RE: *Parking Lot Potholes*
      Sr. Software Engineer

I would like to alert you to the growing number of potholes in the employee parking lot. The hazard is severe for all, and I think they should be fixed. I'm particularly concerned now that most of the snow has melted. This has left large pools of stagnant water in the holes. These mini-swamps can become a breeding ground for mosquitoes and create the potential for a major malaria epidemic that could spread throughout the state. Until these potholes are repaired, the company risks the health of its staff and the community at large.

I would appreciate your correcting this situation before spring breeding begins.

Incredulous over Bertha's focus on malaria rather than tires and axles, Hollister Adams could barely maintain his composure as he dictated the following reply:

TO: Bertha Weiler   DATE: March 4, 1991
*   Sr. Software Engineer*

FROM: Hollister Adams, V.P.   RE: March 1, 1991 Memo
*   Administrative Services*

Thank you for calling our attention to the potholes. We agree that they pose a problem and will have them repaired by no later than April 15.

Please be assured that there is no immediate concern for contracting malaria. The Vermont State Health Department has informed us that they haven't received any reported cases of malaria in the past 223 years.

We appreciate your patience and promise to have a crew out to repair the potholes as soon as possible.

We compliment Mr. Adams for avoiding the temptation to belittle Bertha's concerns and for **Panel Comments** responding to her with dignity. He went a long way in retaining the good will of a highly valued employee, despite her irrational fears.

While Berth'a focus on possible malaria as a result of the potholes is unlikely to create any Legal Comments legal problems, her memo did put the company on notice of the existence of the potholes. Any personal injury or property damage due to the unrepaired potholes is likely to be very expensive for the company. Once an employer is on notice of a defect on its premises (e.g., pothole, broken staircase, etc.), prudence dictates that it be repaired as quickly as possible, not within the leisurely six-week period suggested by Mr. Adams.

HOODWINKED

Mattie came in at 6:30 one morning to review salary actions for merits and promotions. She was a little startled when the phone rang at such an early hour.

"Human Resources, Mattie Kurtz speaking," she answered efficiently.

"Oh, good, Mattie, I thought you might be in. It's 9:30 here. I'm out east on vacation, and I need a special favor," the voice on the other end explained.

Mattie put her pen down and made a sour face. "What does the great white business editor want this time?" she speculated. "Remain professional," she reminded herself as she postured her response.

"Yes, Alex, what did you need?"

"Mattie, you know we've been trying to find a reporter to replace Myron Chester. Well, I've found this terrific guy. I interviewed him right before I left for vacation, and I'd like to get him started the first of next week. Now I know you like to do a thorough reference check on all prospective candidates, but could we make an exception this time and waive the formal investigation?" he asked.

"Alex, you know that's risky. Besides, what if . . ."

"Mattie," he interrupted, "I have copies of all his work. The guy has written pieces for the *Atlantic Monthly, The New York Times*—really fine stuff. I just don't want to take a chance of losing this guy. I want to make him an offer today. Besides, he had several of his former employers call me. They all said they hated to lose him."

"Alex, I don't really like this," Mattie countered.

"I know, Mattie, but I really would appreciate your making an exception this time. My assistant editor, Don Sowald, has all the copies of his portfolio. You can look through the material if you want."

"Okay, Alex," Mattie conceded, "but if there's a problem with this guy, it's on your head. What's his name?"

"Barton Chambers. You're a peach, Mattie. Thanks."

"Oh, yuk," Mattie grimaced. "'You're a peach,'" she mimicked disparagingly. "He's such a chauvinistic jerk."

She hung up the phone and returned to her paperwork.

Mattie wasn't surprised when, two months later, Alex was in her office. "Mattie, we need to fire Barton Chambers."

"Barton Chambers? You mean our 'on-the-brink-of-winning-the-Pulitzer-Prize, Barton Chambers?'" she queried sarcastically.

"Mattie, the guy is weird, and he's getting on my nerves. His most recent shenanigan was the last straw. I want him out of here today," Alex insisted.

Mattie was enjoying this. Alex—the pompous, women-hating, know-it-all editor—was asking her to dig him out of a major screw-up that she had warned him could happen. "How delicious!" she relished secretly. Should she stretch this out and make him squirm? No, she would wait until she heard all the facts. Then she'd decide. Maintaining her professional posture, she replied, "Well, Alex, you'll have to give me all the details so we can build a case. What type of documentation do you have?"

———————◦◦◦◦———————

Alex had been keeping a file on Barton ever since his co-workers started complaining about Barton walking around the office barefoot. Patty Larson, who worked the legislative beat was one of the first to complain.

"Alex, I think something is strange about Barton," Patty began.

"Why, Patty, what exactly do you mean?" Alex patronized.

"Well, Barton is just weird."

"Weird is all encompassing, Patty. Be more specific. Can you give me an example? How can I help him if I don't have specifics?"

"Well, okay," she started to disclose. "Did you know he sometimes walks around the office barefoot? Now that's weird!"

"Yes, I've noticed that," Alex said. "Go on."

"The other day, he asked if he could borrow my brush. Can you believe that, my brush! Who borrows someone else's brush? I don't even like to loan my brush to my sister. So I said to him, 'Gee Barton, I don't seem to have a spare one available,' hoping he would get the hint. But, that wasn't enough. He started rifling through my purse, pulled out my brush, and said, 'Here's a brush, Patty, this will do fine.'"

Patty took a moment to catch her breath. "Alex, he went through my purse. What person, let alone a man, goes through a woman's purse? And then, there's my privacy. I think something's wrong with him."

Alex found the purse incident very disturbing and the business about walking around barefoot annoying.

"Okay, Patty, I'll talk to him, and see if we can get him to refrain from invading your privacy."

"Thanks, Alex, but you really ought to talk to some of the others. I don't want to carry tales that I can't personally substantiate, but maybe you should talk to Rod or John."

"Okay, I will. Is there anything else I should know," he asked.

"Nope, that's it," Patty said and promptly left Alex's office.

Alex spotted Rod in the newsroom and motioned to him to step in his office. "Rod, give me your opinion of our newest reporter, Barton Chambers. How do you think he's doing?"

"Well, I haven't paid much attention to his stuff. I just think he's odd."

"Could you give me an example, Rod?"

Rod thought for a moment. "He drops by my house, unannounced, at odd hours or inconvenient times. I have a wife and children, and he just rings the doorbell, invites himself to dinner, and hangs around for hours playing with my kids."

"What about at work, Rod?"

"At work, hmmmm . . . . He always borrows money and then forgets to pay it back—you know, a dollar here, five dollars there—or he'll make some stupid or inappropriate comment. I just can't recall anything specific."

At this point Alex was not sure he wanted to correct Barton's behavior. Barton was still on probation, although legally that didn't much matter. State law permitted termination of an employee for no reason, as long as the employee couldn't prove discrimination. Barton was white, male, and under forty, so Alex was pretty much home free. However, as a matter of practice, the company usually applied its progressive discipline policy, except in probationary cases. Whatever Alex decided, he'd have to get Mattie involved. That was the worst of it.

While Alex was contemplating his alternatives, Bill Jones, the office administrator, asked to see him.

"Alex, we've got an unusually high phone bill here. Quite a few calls seem to be coming from Barton's extension. Did you have him on a special assignment?"

"No, Bill, he's been writing features on local businesses. Where are these calls?"

"All over the country."

"All over the country? Like where?"

"New York, Florida, Illinois, Washington, Oregon . . . there's about one hundred dollars' worth of calls."

"Were these calls made after hours?"

"Nope, during company time."

"Do me a favor, Bill. Research a few of these calls and find out if they know our Barton Chambers."

"When do you need this?"

"ASAP!" Alex directed.

Bill reported back to Alex by the end of the week. He made ten random calls, three of which connected to the main switchboard of major newspapers, so there was no way of proving that Barton actually made the calls. The remaining seven calls were made to Barton's friends and relatives.

"That's my ticket!" Alex smiled, as he read the report. The next morning he showed up in Mattie's office.

Alex pulled out his file. "Of course I have documentation, Mattie," he said as he slid the manila folder across her desk. She read the reports. "Okay, Alex, you've got a solid case. Let me take care of a few things with payroll. I'll be ready to handle this at 1:00 today. Arrange for your secretary to clean out his desk while he's in the exit interview with us. Let's keep this short and sweet—no longer than fifteen minutes," she instructed him.

Alex and Barton entered Mattie's office promptly at the appointed time. Mattie politely shook Barton's hand and wasted no time explaining the problem and presenting the evidence. She indicated that his office manners and behavior were unbusinesslike. She also pointed to the phone records and the report, informing him that personal use of company telephone for long-distance calls was unauthorized and constituted theft. Barton was to be terminated as of this date. His final paycheck was being processed and would be sent to his home.

As Mattie went through her spiel, she noticed that Barton's physical appearance began to alter. His cheeks flushed slightly, then turned to bright crimson. His eyes widened, narrowed, and then widened again, erupting into a fierce blaze. Before she had finished, he sprang out of his chair and started pacing. With a crazed expression overtaking his face, he began shouting furiously at the wall.

"Do these people realize what they have done to me? Firing me from a major metropolitan newspaper! What will that look like on my record? No one will ever hire me now. I'll be doomed to flipping hamburgers for the rest of my life. How could they do this to me? Well, I just won't accept it. I'll just stay until I can find another job."

"Barton," Mattie injected, "I'm afraid you don't have that option." She flashed a wink at Alex. "Please sit down so that we can finish up our business."

With an incredulous look, Barton turned up the velocity on his pace. "Sit down? I can't sit down. Who could sit down?" He pivoted in Alex's direction. "Alex, could you sit down if I were firing you?"

Alex winced. Barton kept stomping behind Alex's chair, hurling his arms in every direction. Normally, Mattie might have been slightly frightened, but Alex's reactions distracted her fears. Barton's histrionics caused him to occasionally graze the back of Alex's chair. Mattie could see that Alex was growing increasingly uncomfortable with each bump. The first sign was an involuntary tic that Alex developed over his right eye. This tic graduated to a full-blown twitch when it traded places with his left cheek. Her thoughts gleefully applauded when she saw his twitches journey to his seat, setting Alex in motion as he danced the old ants-in-your-pants with metronomic precision, shifting from side to side in two-second intervals.

It was clear the whole situation had Alex totally unnerved. "Ah, there is a God," she chuckled to herself. "What a wonderful chance to let some of your hot air escape, jerk-off," she continued thinking as she watched Barton's tirade behind Alex's back become more and more incoherent.

Neither Mattie nor Alex attempted to interrupt Barton as he expressed his outrage. Eventually, Barton's battery wore down. Defeated and speechless, he flopped back in his chair and stared vacantly at Mattie. After a few blinks, Mattie broke the silence.

"Barton, Alex's secretary has gathered all of your belongings. She has them ready for you. Before you leave, however, you'll need to turn in your company ID, please."

As though under hypnosis, Barton reached into his back pocket and produced the ID.

"Thank you, Barton. Alex will escort you out now."

Alex shot a frightened glance to Mattie. Mattie nodded and signaled with her eyes that everything would be okay. Reluctantly, Alex rose from his seat and walked out of the office with Barton. When Alex could see Barton's silhouette disappear from view, he breathed an exhausted, weary sigh. He turned to the elevator and looked at his watch. This fifteen-minute termination interview had turned into an hour-long drama, one he never wanted to sit through again.

———————◦◦◦◦———————

The next morning, Mattie's secretary informed her that the Chicago School of Journalism was on the phone.

"Ms. Kurtz," the voice on the other end said, "do you have a Barton Chambers still in your employ?"

"No, he's no longer with us," Mattie responded cautiously, but her curiosity was piqued.

"What a relief," the caller sighed. "Then I guess you found out he faked his credentials."

Not wanting to reveal her utter surprise and the embarrassment of yesterday's fiasco, Mattie replied cagily, "Oh, do you have some additional information on that?"

"Well, when he provided us with this beautiful portfolio, we were all naturally very impressed. We just thought it a trifle strange that a man so young and obviously unsophisticated could have accomplished such a broad spectrum of work at his age. So, we decided to track down the original work on microfilm in our library. We discovered that he was not the author at all. From what we could piece together, he obtained originals of the work, masked out the by-line, and replaced it with his name using matching press type. Then he photocopied the articles and presented them as his own. Actually, his only real newspaper job prior to working for you was at the Pocatello *Gazette*."

Mattie's mouth hung open as she discovered the truth. "To think," she said to herself, "that I actually felt sort of guilty about having to fire this guy. What a dirtbag."

Returning her thoughts to her caller, she politely commented, "We certainly do appreciate your update. We really don't have much to add, but we'll be sure to inform any other prospective employers to validate his portfolio. Thanks so much for calling."

Outraged, Mattie immediately called Alex.

"Alex, didn't we receive a national award for crack investigative reporting last year?"

"Why yes, Mattie, why do you ask?"

"Well, I just found out from the Chicago School of Journalism that all of those sterling credentials Barton gave you were faked!"

"What?"

"That's right, faked. The only other newspaper job he had was at some Podunk paper in Idaho."

"But what about all the references I talked to?"

"Didn't you tell me they called you?"

"Well, yes, they did."

"Well, our buddy Barton no doubt had his friends call you and tell you they were the editor of those newspapers. That's probably what all those long distance calls were for. He was getting ready to apply elsewhere and was alerting his friends to call prospective employers as references. Who knows, he may even have faked his voice and provided his own reference."

Mattie was still fuming and hadn't had her full say. "But do we, ace reporters that we are, thoroughly check out his references? Nooooooo, we throw our silly procedures to the wind. We're confident about this guy, we're sure he's gonna put us right up there with *The New York Times*." she mocked.

"Do we notice that his work seems rather ordinary or maybe even sub-standard?" she kept on. "Of course not! No, instead we focus on minutia and fire the guy because he doesn't want to wear his shoes and borrows somebody's brush!"

Winding up for the last pitch, and this one was guaranteed to be a spitball, Mattie fired, "And, Alex, I'm warning you, if you ever involve me in this kind of crap again, I swear I'll call every one of your editor buddies and make you the butt of every cocktail joke they tell at your damn conventions. And one more thing, don't you ever— and I mean ever—ask me to make an exception for you again," she fumed, crashing the phone down with the receiver still smoking.

 We can certainly understand Mattie's anger and frustration at being talked into making an exception that backfired. However, given the behavior of Barton Chambers, a more prudent course of action might have been to have alerted the security guards to be ready to escort Chambers out. Sending Alex out to the elevator with someone in Chamber's mental state might have had some unfortunate consequences. In these emotionally charged situations, it is best to err on the side of caution.

Clearly, Mattie and Alex erred by not verifying his credentials in advance. Mattie's suggestion **Legal Comments** that "if anything happened, it would fall on

Alex's head" is not entirely correct. If the obviously unstable and deceitful employee had injured someone or damaged property while working, the newspaper may well incur legal liability.

9
TRAGIC SOULS

It's nearly impossible to predict a person's response to excessive stress or terrifying fear. Even the healthiest of us may temporarily withdraw or lash out in anger during intensely difficult times. Unfortunately, some people become so paralyzed by fear that they retreat into a world of denial. Others take the path of self-destruction. For them, it's easier than facing the pain. In either case, the ending is almost always tragic.

WHERE THERE'S SIN THERE'S SUFFERING

Hank Corcoran, the vice president of security knew he had his work cut out for him when he received a complaint from the insurance department that Thursday. The complaint alleged fraudulent activities of their newly-hired agent, Dan Gorginston. The document stated that four years earlier, Dan sold an elderly immigrant couple two single premium life policies totaling $30,000. He purchased these policies from another insurance carrier whom he represented at the time. However, when Dan changed companies, he forged the couple's signatures and cancelled their policies without their knowledge. Then he replaced their policies with term insurance from his new company. This enabled him to pocket the difference of nearly $29,000, plus earn a second sales commission on the two new term policies.

Dan probably could have kept this information from the couple for many years. But the original carrier wrote the couple a letter asking why they decided to cancel rather than borrow against their policy, since it was already paid up. This prompted the couple to call the carrier and say they were unaware of the transaction. When they discovered what actually happened, the couple filed a complaint with the state insurance department.

Hank chewed on his pipe while mulling over the complaint. Then he keyed Dan's name into his PC. "Location: 2099 Avalon Road" flashed across the screen. "I think I'll go out and pay him an unexpected visit first thing next week," he said to himself and called his travel agency to make reservations. Next he called the corporate attorneys and set up a meeting to brief them.

The following Monday, Hank walked into Dan's office and was greeted by his secretary. "Hi, I'm Hank Corcoran from the home office," he smiled. "We're visiting agents in the region this week. Is Dan in?"

"Oh, gee, Mr. Corcoran, did Dan know you were coming? He's out until three this afternoon."

"No, he didn't," Hank answered. "Occasionally, we drop in to do a routine check of our new agents' offices just to see how they're getting along." He looked at his watch, "Hmmm, it's two o'clock now. If you don't mind, I'd like to do my facilities check around the office. By the time I'm done, Dan should be back."

The secretary seemed somewhat uncertain, so Hank showed her his official-looking clipboard with the company logo and a loss prevention safety check-off sheet he had cleverly inserted. "Oh, sure, go ahead then," she nodded. "Do you need my help, or can I continue with my work?"

"Oh, thanks for the offer," Hank smiled, "but I've done a zillion of these, and most offices are laid out the same. I think I'll be just fine."

The secretary returned to her work, and Hank appeared as though he was taking inventory. He noticed that the typewriter Dan's secretary was using was stamped, "Quartermaster, U.S. Army." Hank figured it was surplussed but noted the serial number on his list. As he walked about the office, Hank's suspicions grew when he found two other typewriters hidden in a storeroom. They bore the same army stamp. He copied down their serial numbers and immediately checked the government listings in the phone book. There was a local army base in the vicinity.

Hank was sitting at Dan's desk noting the number of the local army base when Dan returned. Hank stood up and introduced himself.

"Welcome, Hank. What a pleasant surprise," Dan charmed. "Susie just told me you were here doing some kind of safety check or something."

"Unfortunately, Dan, it's more than that," Hank began evenly, "we have a little problem."

"Well, all problems are solvable. What can I do to help?" Dan offered, doubling his charm.

"It seems we have a complaint from the state insurance department that requires our response," said Hank as he handed Dan the report.

Dan quickly scanned the report and handed it back to Hank. "Oh, this must be a mistake. I've never heard of these people," he denied.

"Well, I think you better get yourself a lawyer before you say any more, Dan," Hank suggested and offered the report back to Dan. "You'll probably need this for reference."

Dan begrudgingly accepted the report and set his briefcase down.

Then Hank added, "Dan, I'm also here to inform you that you are temporarily suspended from writing any further policies until the matter is resolved. We are sending in Allen Markham to service your business. He will be here at 8:00 A.M. tomorrow morning. Please hand over all sets of your keys. The locksmith will be changing the locks this afternoon. You are to vacate immediately."

"Do . . . do I at least get to take my personal belongings out of my desk?" Dan asked.

"Sorry, no," Hank responded unemotionally. "We can't take the chance of any evidence being removed. We'll arrange for you to have your things after everything has been gone through by our internal auditors."

Dan was so stunned that he grabbed his briefcase and started to leave.

"Excuse me, Dan," Hank reminded him, "your keys please."

"Oh, right," Dan remarked, pulling two keys off his key ring. Then he turned toward the door.

"Dan, one more thing," Hank added.

"What now?" Dan responded through clenched teeth as he grew more and more irritated.

Hank pointed to the briefcase. "Are there any company documents in the briefcase?"

"Uh . . . well, yes, I just sold a policy," Dan stammered.

"Then empty it," Hank said, pointing to the chair.

Dan clutched his briefcase to his chest and began to move toward the door. Hank, anticipating his reaction, had positioned himself in the doorway.

Dan angrily threw the briefcase on the nearest chair, pushed Hank aside, and stomped out of the office. Hank could hear Dan's car roar out of the parking lot. Then Hank walked to the outer office where Dan's secretary was fully engrossed in her work. She was clearly oblivious of what had just transpired.

"Excuse me," Hank interupted, "but I don't think you ever told me your name."

"Susie," she smiled. "Susie Stratton."

"Susie, I need to inform you of some changes that are going to take place."

"Yes . . ." she responded somewhat warily. She was very young and inexperienced but loved her job. She began to get frightened that the company was going to lay her off.

"Dan will not be in the office for awhile, and he may not be returning at all. We are sending a substitute agent to handle his business. His name is Allen Markham."

"Why, what's wrong?" she asked with a concerned look on her face. "Is Dan all right?"

"I can't go into detail right now. When do you report for work?" Hank asked.

"At 8:00 A.M.," she responded. "Am I being laid off?"

"No, this has nothing to do with you. Don't worry," Hank assured her. "However, do not report for work until 9:00 A.M. tomorrow, to allow Allen to get settled."

"How do I fill out my time card?" she asked. "I can't afford to lose hours."

"You have my approval to fill it out with regular hours. Don't worry, you won't have to make up the time."

"Are you sure? Dan was very strict about my time."

"Typical," Hank thought. "He'll nickel and dime his secretary while he rips off everyone else." Then Hank responded, "Yes, I'm sure."

"Can't you tell me anything more?" she asked.

"I'm afraid not—it's confidential company business. But everything will be fine. A locksmith will be here soon to change the locks. When he arrives, I would like you to leave. And, again, don't worry. You'll be paid for the full day. Finish up whatever you were working on. The rest can wait until tomorrow."

The locksmith arrived, and the secretary left as Hank instructed. While the locksmith worked, Hank decided to call the number he found for the army base. He inquired if the army had recently surplussed any electric typewriters and provided the staff with the serial numbers. His inquiry revealed that the typewriters were reported stolen from the base six months ago. Hank informed the staff that he had spotted the equipment at Dan's office and told them they could pick up the typewriters any time. Then he gave them Dan's home number and address.

Based on the evidence gathered by the company's investigators, the state insurance department revoked Dan's license. Concurrently, the military began to move in on Dan regarding the stolen typewriters. All this was too much for Dan to bear. He took his life rather than face imprisonment.

Panel Comments Although we all regret the tragic outcome of this case, we also recognize that both Hank Corcoran and the company had very serious responsibilities to their clients. Hank acted properly by responding quickly and using legal counsel, but he should have given more thought to the human side—both for Dan and his secretary. Hank's mystery with the secretary caused her to have undue concern for her job, and Hank missed an opportunity to glean some important information about the operation. Because of Hank's mishandling of the employee relations component, the new agent will have a much tougher time getting the office to resume a business-as-usual environment.

Legal Comments One of the issues posed by this story is the extent to which an employer can lawfully search an employee's desk, office, briefcase, etc. While the constitutional prohibition against warrantless searches and seizures generally applies only to governmental agents, some state constitutions and judicial decisions have restricted a private employer's rights in this regard as well. It would have been desirable for Hank to have familiarized himself with the extent of his authority to conduct a search before doing so. While the law of each jurisdiction varies, a rule of thumb is that the closer you get to the employee's "person," the greater is the employee's expectation of privacy and, hence, the greater the risk of liability for the employer who engages in searches of employees or their property.

TWIN FATALITIES

"Lila, could you come to my office in a few minutes? I need to discuss a new processing project with you," Shelly asked with a smile as she stopped by Lila's desk.

"I can come right now if you want," Lila responded, always eager to please.

"Fine, then let's walk together," Shelly said as she watched Lila push herself away from her desk. It seemed Lila had been gaining weight lately, and as Shelly observed her more closely, Lila's walk had taken on a slight waddle.

"No," she thought, "couldn't be. She's never missed a day of work, never complained about anything. She's so shy, too. I can't even imagine her with a man, although she is kind of attractive," Shelly further mused.

By the time they reached Shelly's office, she dismissed her thoughts of Lila's weight problems and focused on the business at hand.

After the meeting, Lila gathered all the project data and returned to her desk. In her typical, steadfast manner, Lila worked on all the details and completed the assignment in two weeks—one week ahead of schedule. When Lila walked into Shelly's office on Tuesday, she smiled and quietly asked, "Do you have a moment, Shelly?"

Shelly had been out of town for the past week and had arrived home late Monday night. So when Shelly looked up at Lila standing before her, she was somewhat startled. Lila appeared to be her former lithe self. Since Lila was so private about her personal life, Shelly didn't feel comfortable about making a comment. Instead she replied, "Sure, Lila, have a seat."

"I finished up your project a week early," she began nonchalantly. "Are there any other special projects you need me to work on? I have the time."

"That's wonderful, Lila!" Shelly beamed. "As a matter of fact, I do. It's some special research for the Norton account."

"Just tell me what you need to have done, and I'll get right to it!"

"Boy, I wish I had three just like you, Lila," Shelly said sincerely and began to explain the project.

In the meantime, unbeknownst to Shelly, Charles Gavin, the human resources manager, was investigating a complaint about Lila. Several employees had noticed a malodorous scent emanating from the trunk of Lila's car. Charles went to the parking lot early that morning to smell for himself. The stench was so strong and so foreign that instinct told him to involve the local authorities. When the police arrived, they looked worried and said they needed to obtain a search warrant. Several hours later, they returned with a warrant and Detective Bradford. Together they opened the trunk of Lila's car. Much to their horror, they discovered two dead infants wrapped up in blankets in Lila's trunk. It appeared as though the infants were not full term, perhaps two to three months premature. Pictures were taken, and the remains were immediately removed and taken to the morgue.

Charles asked the police not to apprehend Lila in front of her co-workers. He would arrange for Lila to come to the Human Resources Department. Then he called Shelly.

"Shelly, this is Charles Gavin. We have a problem with Lila. I can't go into details right now, but I'll fill you in later. Will you ask her to accompany you to my office? Just tell her it has to do with a project you're working on."

Shelly didn't like the mystery. It was uncharacteristic of Charles to keep her in the dark. "Charles, what is this all about? I don't like lying to my people."

"Trust me, Shelly," his voice almost pleaded. "I'll tell you everything when you get here."

"Okay," she said reluctantly, "but I don't like this."

Charles had asked the detective to accompany him to his office. He asked that the uniformed police remain out of sight. He was worried about frightening employees and wanted to hear Lila's explanation.

When Shelly brought Lila to Charles's office, Detective Bradford was seated at the conference table. "Please come in, Lila."

Lila edged closer to Shelly. She was clearly uncomfortable and started to shake.

"Lila, this is Detective Bradford. Detective Bradford, this is Lila Callow and her supervisor, Shelly Sexton," Charles continued. They all nodded to each other and took seats around the conference table in Charles's office.

"Lila, we had some complaints about an odor coming from the trunk of your car," Charles began. "It was so unusual that I called in some experts, and they told me I had to get it opened to look."

"You opened the trunk of my car without my permission?" Lila blurted. "What right did you have to do that? How dare you! My car is private!" Lila started to cry.

Shelly was shocked. She had never seen Lila ever lose her cool, much less express any form of real emotion.

"Do you know what we found, Lila?" Charles asked compassionately.

"Yes," she sobbed. "My babies."

"Her babies!" Shelly thought, clutching her stomach in a sudden wave of nausea. "My God, what has she done?"

Charles handed Lila a box of tissues and asked, "Can you tell us how they got there?"

"I put them there," she whimpered.

"Why, Lila? Why did you do that?" he asked gently.

"I . . . I didn't know what else to do," she sputtered.

"What do you mean?"

"On . . . on . . . Friday night I started cramping and bleeding."

"Did you go to the hospital?"

"No, I couldn't tell anyone I was pregnant."

"This poor kid had these babies alone in her apartment?"
Shelly silently envisioned. "I can't imagine how horrible that
was for her! What was she so afraid of that would cause her
to endure this?"

"Why not?" Charles probed further.

"My father is a minister, and . . . and . . . if he knew I
had loved a man, he would have beaten me again . . . like
when he found me kissing Bobby," she gasped. "So I
couldn't tell. I was still trying to decide what to do, but I
thought I had time."

"No wonder she never let anyone know about her
personal life. Her father must have been a monster to cause
her such fear," Shelly imagined.

"What do you mean?" Charles asked further.

"You know, like go off to one of those homes. I was
saving my vacation up so I could."

"That's true," Shelly reflected, "she hasn't taken a day all
year."

"Then no one would know. I never saw a doctor, so I
didn't even know there would be two," Lila weeped. "But
the babies . . . they just came early. I wasn't expecting
them. I never even heard them cry . . . ." She sobbed
uncontrollably and repeated hysterically, "I never even
heard them cry."

"So what were you going to do with your babies?"
Charles asked next.

"I hadn't figured it out. I haven't been able to look at
them since I put them in the trunk."

"I can't believe this," Shelly's mind flashed to earlier this
morning. "She just walked into my office this morning
asking for more work—she had time to take on a new
project. My God, how is this woman even functioning?"

"Would you like to see a doctor now to make sure
you're okay?"

"Yes," she responded.

"I'm sure this has been very difficult for you. How about seeing another doctor to help you cope with this emotionally?" he urged.

"I suppose," she uttered quietly.

"And your parents, would you like us to call them?"

"No!" she said emphatically.

"Okay, we'll respect that, Lila."

"First we're going to send you to the company Medical Department to get Dr. Janson's opinion on whether you need medication or hospitalization. Then he'll select a doctor to talk with you to help you through this problem. Does that sound okay to you?"

"That's okay."

"Shelly, would you escort Lila to Medical and wait for her?"

"Sure," Shelly said, still shocked by what she had just learned but feeling overwhelming compassion for Lila.

When they left, Charles turned to Detective Bradford and asked, "Do you think we have any real intentional foul play here?"

"Probably not," he responded, "but we'll have to conduct an autopsy to determine the real cause of death and the age of the infants. I think Lila's going to need to be institutionalized to help her through the emotional trauma. She clearly gets no comfort from her folks."

"Are you going to charge her?"

"Not yet, not until I have the autopsy report."

"Can we keep this quiet so that if the autopsy report clears her, she doesn't have to experience further pain and humiliation?"

"Well, there are some other legal issues, but I'll do my best."

Detective Bradford honored his word. The autopsy report cleared Lila of intentionally causing her infants' deaths and not a word was leaked to the press. The doctors determined that Lila was undergoing severe emotional and psychological problems and required hospitalization to improve her mental health. Physically, she was fine and required no care other than preventive antibiotics.

Lila never returned to the company, but the company fully covered all her medical and hospital expenses until she was released.

Panel Comments This is truly a tragic case—for the premature babies who never had a chance, for Lila herself, and for the woman and man in the company who handled the situation. The horror of the situation obviously concerns the first two, but it's important to note here that this was most certainly a gut-wrenching experience for the two company representatives. They clearly did everything that caring human beings in a business environment would be expected to do. It was appropriate and generous for the company to take care of Lila's medical expenses. We also applaud the human resources manager for keeping Lila's privacy and dignity in mind by asking the police not to confront her in the presence of her co-workers and by talking with her as kindly as possible.

The detective also showed his humanity and professionalism when he treated the "suspect" with compassion and didn't rush into some *Dirty Harry* interrogation and arrest. The actions of the people around Lila don't make the tragedy any less awful, but they do make one believe in the benefit of treating people with respect and trying to help rather than finger the blame without knowing the facts.

Legal Comments Employers are expert in their own business. However, they are not expert in handling situations of this type. Thus, it was prudent for the company to call for assistance from the appropriate agency—in this case, the local police.

10
MASTERS
OF INVENTION

This rare breed of workplace wizards has the uncanny ability to immobilize a problem and make it disappear. When challenged with difficult, sensitive, and life-threatening situations, these masters magically reach into a bag of tricks to pull out illusions and alter perceptions. Their unsung sorcery has saved many faces and sometimes lives as well. Few outside the inner circle have been privy to secrets they are about to share.

RADIATING FEAR

Reed was worried as picketing employees jeered and shouted outside his window. The strike at the chemical plant had been going on longer than usual. Management and union officials continued to negotiate, hammering out each part of the contract with slow deliberate motions. Progress had been too slow for the employees. They were angry at their union representatives and furious with management. Tempers grew shorter as each day passed. With Christmas less than twenty days away, Reed instinctively knew that they would have to settle soon or something would blow.

The morning's mail confirmed Reed's fears. It contained an anonymous threat on management lives and a promise to sabotage plant equipment. Since the plant produced hazardous chemicals, he could not dismiss the letter. Sabotage meant potential loss of employee lives, destruction of millions of dollars of equipment, and danger to the surrounding community. If someone intentionally tried to blow up the building, chemicals could ignite and release a toxic cloud into the atmosphere. Reed would need to alert the state police so they could plan an evacuation if it were necessary.

Three sides of the plant were well-guarded and protected by a twelve-foot barbed wire fence. The west side was worrisome. There was no fence at that entrance, and Reed was concerned that someone would try to slip in. He didn't want to hire armed guards, because the west side faced a busy street and onlookers would become curious. The whole thing would attract too much attention and would be bad public relations. The last thing Reed wanted was for the company to appear as though it were using Gestapo tactics. He needed a simple, effective solution to keep the picketers away from that west entrance.

Reed smiled as the answer came. Since it was 1971 and the community was rural, virtually none of the employees knew what satellite communication dishes looked like, much less their purpose. Reed got on the phone and located a manufacturer. He explained his need to the manufacturer and his urgency for immediate delivery.

The next morning the dish was on its way. The regular band of picketers stopped their chanting as they saw the flatbed truck approach and hiss its air brakes at them with its ominous-looking cargo towering above them. A crane was engaged to set the dish down a few feet in front of the west wall of the building. The big snout projecting from the dish pointed directly across the expansive lawn and toward the picketers who marched along the sidewalk.

The delivery company's crew busily appeared as though they were installing and connecting massive wires to a junction box attached to the wall. The picketers' curiosity kept them quiet for over an hour. Once all the wires were "connected," Reed came out with a bull horn in hand.

"Gentlemen, as you can see we have just installed a new rodent control device," he announced. "The company has recently experienced a severe rodent problem along its west perimeter. This equipment is designed to be sensitive to motion. If any object gets within forty feet of the west perimeter, the device is programmed to emit radioactive waves that will fan out to about two hundred fifty feet. We do not know what impact these waves have on humans, but research has shown they effectively cause sterility in animals. We caution you to avoid getting anywhere near the west wall if you value your reproductive organs. We are not sure about any other damage that might happen, since this equipment has not been tested for any length of time on humans. So, for your personal safety, be advised to conduct all picketing at the front gates. I am about to engage the equipment, so I'd appreciate your moving from the area immediately. Thank you for your cooperation."

The strikers grabbed their placards and ran to the front gate. Throughout the duration of the strike, outside monitors revealed that no one ever came near the west wall again.

This ingenious solution seems to be a **Panel Comments** successful, short-term public relations alternative. However, there are some very real negative possibilities in the long term. As time marches on and the ruse becomes apparent, the work force is likely to discredit anything management tells them in the future.

While the company's activity might be viewed by the National Labor Relations Board as a **Legal Comments** technical interference with the protected rights of employees to picket, that is a fairly remote possibility.

A BRILLIANT BLUFF

Joe Matson walked into the conference room. The good old boys were all seated around the table. Their faces were grim and concerned. Joe took his seat and settled in.

Glenn Jansen, vice president of operations, led the discussion. "We're concerned about Stella Trottier. She's one of the customer service trainees sent up from the Augusta district. Apparently, she's gotten very wild during her stay at the Ramada, and we've had a number of complaints from the other trainees housed at the motel. She's out drinking every night and has been entertaining a variety of local boys in her room. We just can't have that kind of girl working for us. Our company has an image to maintain in the community. Since you're the human resources manager, we need your help in firing her."

"I see," Joe commented. "Let me ask you a few questions first. How is Stella's performance on the job?"

"Well, I don't know. Who here can speak to that?" Glenn asked.

"I can," Mike Steel replied. Mike was the sales manager in charge of telemarketing and customer service.

"So how's her work?" Joe repeated.

"Fine—actually very good—when she's in the office," Mike responded.

"What do you mean 'when she's in the office'?" Joe asked. "Is she missing time on the job?"

"Oh, I didn't mean that. She's always here on time and finishes all her work. She's picked up the new training very well. What I meant was that she's out of control when she leaves here."

"And you think that we should fire her because you disapprove of her life style?" Joe asked.

"Well, yes. She's setting a bad example for the rest of the team. It's bad for morale. None of our girls behave like that, and we don't want to see it."

"Absolutely," chimed Doug Bentson, the controller. "We don't want trash like that around here."

The group was all happily agreeing with themselves when Joe decided to drop the first shoe.

"Gentlemen, I want you to know that I have been aware of the Stella Trottier situation. The motel manager from the Ramada and I have been in close contact for over a week about this. Now we can fire Stella if you would like, but I want to let you know that if we do, we are sure to be slapped with a sex discrimination case. From your own admissions, her performance is above satisfactory. What she chooses to do when she is not on company time is up to her. Both of these facts will go against us if we fire her for the reason you just gave me. I can also assure you that the Equal Employment Opportunity Commission will rule in her favor, and the company will pay a stiff settlement. And remember, *that* settlement will affect our bottom line and ultimately our bonuses—but that's up to you. However, if you insist that we fire her, it's important to bear in mind that there's more to this than money. A sex discrimination suit will lead to a major investigation. That means I will have to turn my files over to the feds, and we'll have to get sworn statements from the manager of the Ramada."

"So what's the big deal, Joe?" Glenn interrupted.

Joe was prepared for this. He had suspected the nature of this meeting and wanted to avoid the time and expense of an unnecessary civil rights suit, especially since it would involve so much of his time. He also knew that this group could be as inflexible as a rusty suit of armor once they decided an employee had to go. So, before responding, Joe opened a file he had handy, secretly crossed his fingers, and tucked his hand from view.

"Well, it so happens that I've been aware of this situation since Stella's third day here. So, I asked the Ramada manager to keep a record of all the car license plates parked in front of her door. He gave me that list yesterday, and I found something very interesting. One of the license plate numbers he noted comes from a company-owned vehicle assigned to one of you in this room," Joe lied.

"Now if I were to turn this over for investigation," Joe continued, "there would be a whole lot of explaining to do."

Joe took a long pause and locked eyes with each manager for a split second, hoping his bluff would hold. "Here's what I suggest instead. Stella has only one more week of training. When she returns to Augusta, she can go back to live with her mom and dad who'll keep a tight rein on her activities. We'll still have a good employee in the Augusta district, the company's training dollars will be recouped, and we won't have to spend a whole lot of time and money paying a sex discrimination suit, which will embarrass the devil out of one of our officers. How does that sound?"

The room was silent for a few moments. Finally, Glenn nervously cleared his throat and sputtered, "Excellent suggestion, Joe. Is there anyone who objects to this alternative?"

Glenn looked around the room.

No one said a word.

"I guess that concludes our meeting then. Joe, thanks for all your help."

Joe uncrossed his fingers and carefully tucked his papers in his files.

Panel Comments Human resources professionals should be trusted, contributing members of the management team. If they want to maintain their rightful place at the table, they must play by the rules.

Duping management into "doing the right thing" is clearly a violation of those rules. If Joe's peers ever discovered his deceptive tactics, they would no doubt exclude him from participating in future critical business decisions.

I generally agree with Joe Matson. Companies that impose discipline based on employees' off-**Legal Comments** premises conduct run a substantial risk of wrongful discharge and related lawsuits, not to mention the possible embarrassment such a lawsuit might cause.

On the other hand, where an employee is engaging in conduct that may affect performance on the job, an employer has a legitimate basis to take appropriate action (e.g., counseling, warning, etc.) to address the situation, even if the employee's conduct is away from the work place. Moreover, when an employer is housing a group of out-of-town employees for company-related purposes, the company would be within its right to insist that those employees do nothing to damage the company's image and reputation. The key to defusing these potentially explosive situations is often the manner in which they are handled.

UNDISPUTED DRAMA

Jack was reviewing his file on Wilma Carter, an employee in the Receiving Department. The records showed that Wilma had a terrible attendance record and had been counseled several times. Unfortunately, these counseling sessions didn't prevent the attendance problem from recurring. With several oral warnings under her belt and a five-day suspension on her record, Wilma's most recent transgression brought on an official disciplinary hearing. This required the attendance of her union steward and the personnel manager.

As personnel manager, Jack was getting tired of Wilma's constant problem and wanted her fired. However, he knew that his case might be too weak to sustain a termination and that such action would probably cause the union to appeal. Then the case would go to arbitration, which probably would reduce the termination to another five-day suspension. Jack also knew that the standard progressive discipline policy followed the sequence of two oral warnings, a five-day suspension, a thirty-day suspension, and termination. He needed to get a thirty-day suspension on her record so he could be rid of Wilma once and for all without union interference. He was running through his alternative strategies when Pete arrived.

Jack was surprised to see Pete. Pete was the union's business agent, not the steward. The union had been losing membership lately, and Jack figured they must have decided to send in the big guns to rebuild member confidence. Jack stood up to greet Pete and extended his hand with a warm, friendly grasp.

"So, Pete, good to see you."

"You too, Jack. It's been awhile—probably three years. Wasn't it the last contract negotiation?"

"You know, I think you're right. So tell me, Pete, what's brewing? Is the steward off ill?"

"No," Pete said, "I just thought it would be a good idea to come down and handle this one myself. Thought it would be a boost to member morale, you know."

"Sure," Jack confirmed.

Jack was thrilled that Pete was taking over. He knew Pete wasn't as in touch with company policy as the steward, so he remained cool as the conversation proceeded.

"So, Jack, where do you stand on Wilma's case?" Pete asked.

"Well, her attendance record stinks, so I think I'm going to recommend we can her," Jack said, knowing he didn't have enough to make it stick.

"Oh, you can't do that, Jack. Wilma is really a good gal and she's very sorry, but she's been having problems at home. Why don't you just give her a real stern warning?"

"No way. She's already been suspended for five days and that didn't seem to work. I think she should be canned."

"Well, how about you give her a thirty-day suspension?"

This was what Jack was looking for, but he couldn't agree too quickly.

"Naaah, I think we should can her."

"Well, look, I need this one. We'll go into the hearing and you argue strongly that she should be terminated; you yell and scream and all that stuff. Then I'll yell and scream that she should be retained."

"Okay, then what happens?" Jack asked.

"Then we'll agree at the hearing to settle for thirty days. I'll be a hero with Wilma, and she'll tell all the other employees how hard I worked to save her job and didn't let you can her. The whole deal will score big with the members."

"Bingo," Jack thought, "I get my thirty-day suspension on record and Pete will agree not to go to arbitration. This should be easy." However, Jack was not quite prepared for how far Pete was going to carry out his acting debut.

They both walked in the room. Wilma's eyes were downcast, and Pete's hand was on her shoulder giving her a reassuring squeeze.

"Wilma," Jack began, "we've counseled you and warned you and suspended you for your absenteeism. I guess you think this company is a big joke. We can't have employees who don't respect our rules. People like you don't belong here. We're going to have to terminate you."

Wilma gasped and started to cry. She turned to Pete for help as her crying turned into a loud wail.

Pete jumped in immediately. "How dare you talk to one of your employees like she had the emotional make-up of a worm. Don't you have any sense of respect? Who do you think you are, looking down at Wilma through those trifocal, horned-rimmed spectacles? Do you think those glasses give you the right to belittle employees?"

"I don't care what you think. Wilma broke the rules and she pays the price. Our production is down when she isn't on the job, and we don't want to encourage that kind of irresponsibility," Jack retorted.

"Irresponsible? Who's irresponsible? You're putting a woman with three children to feed out on the street for a few extra absences. I think *that's* irresponsible, and it's inexcusable management. You're a low-down, no good, management jerk-off who has nothing to do but push papers all day. Why don't you go out on the line and work some time? Take some time to see who does the real work around here instead of drinking coffee and making decisions that affect the lives of others while you sit in the comfort of your plush offices."

Jack was looking for a way out of this. This was getting out of hand and he was beginning to think that Pete had forgotten the deal they had struck in his office a few minutes earlier. He started to get scared as Pete continued to rant and become increasingly more vicious.

"And furthermore, Mr. high falutin' Personnel Manager, I will fight you every step of the way if you terminate this poor, hard-working woman. I find termination an unacceptable alternative. You'd better come up with something better, or I'll take this thing to arbitration and out of your slimy hands."

At last, Pete gave Jack the opening he needed. He summoned up a stern expression on his face and said firmly, "Don't think your disparaging remarks mean anything to me. I don't need to stoop to your language or your tactics, and I'm not convinced that Wilma will improve. However, I'm not as unreasonable and heartless as you suggest. So, here's my final offer. I'll agree to a thirty-day suspension. Hopefully, she'll have sufficient time to decide if she really wants to work here or not, but that's her absolute last chance."

"Done," said Pete.

Wilma threw her arms around Pete and then thanked Jack profusely for letting her keep her job. Pete put his arm around Wilma and walked her out of the hearing room as he threw a wink over his left shoulder at Jack.

Panel Comments These two are not exactly a couple of role models. The back room, deal-cutting nature of this episode is not to be admired or encouraged. If Jack had simply followed the standard, progressive discipline policy, he should have been able to obtain the thirty-day suspension without compromising his integrity.

Legal Comments Although this general scenario is not uncommon in unionized companies, the specific language and tone Pete employed is uncommon. No manager would need to tolerate that kind of activity.

When dealing with employee problems like attendance, where no single episode is sufficient to warrant substantial discipline or discharge, an employer should take pains to rely on the cumulative effect of the employee's various transgressions or the entire course of conduct. The employer should not focus on the most recent episode as the basis for discipline. Instead, the most recent episode should be treated as the proverbial straw.

11
PETTY PLAINTIFFS

Terminating an employee is always distasteful. At best, the employee takes his lumps and leaves. Unfortunately, we live in a litigious society, so it is all too common for employees to feel that their discharge was wrongful, no matter what the circumstances. They perceive that the corporation has deep pockets, with sufficient reserve to meet their greed. Effective labor counsel can often get frivolous cases dismissed. Sometimes, however, the corporation settles to avoid excessive costs. At worst, an employee successfully pulls off a scam, embarrassing the company while depleting its bottom line.

PERVERSE VERSE

Rob had trouble with Billy from the beginning. First it was minor things, like not fully cleaning up his work station before the next shift arrived or leaving parts of his paperwork incomplete. Billy scowled whenever Rob counseled him. Billy was never good at accepting criticism but would attempt to improve for awhile. Unfortunately, he'd lapse back to the same headstrong behavior. Rob put up with him longer than he should have because Billy was a crack technician. However, on March 18, Rob reached the end of his rope with Billy.

"Billy," Rob began, "I've noticed that you haven't turned in your service report. When can I expect it?"

"When I feel like getting around to it," Billy sniped.

Rob started to redden, but kept calm. "Billy," he began slowly, "I'm afraid I need the report right now. I expect to have it on my desk in five minutes."

Tommy, who considered himself the company's version of Ogden Nash, observed this exchange with glee. He sat at the bench adjacent to Billy, and as soon as the fracas began, he glued his eyes to his oscillator and tuned up his ears. He knew this show would make great material for his next set of verses.

Rob stood at Billy's bench waiting for a response. "Well?" he demanded.

"Get off my ass, Rob," Billy snapped. "You know, Rob, you can be such a shmuck sometimes. Look, you don't need that report right now. You just enjoy getting on my case. Besides, can't you see I'm busy repairing this console? Now, what's more important, a lousy report or getting our customer satisfied?"

Billy's insubordination infuriated Rob. "That's not the point, Billy," Rob began. Rob had endured enough. This was going to be Billy's last outburst. "What *is* the point, Billy my friend, is that you're outta here—TODAY!"

"Good. Fine, fine. I don't give a fuck about this job. I don't need to work for jerks like you," Billy raged, throwing down his tools. "As a matter of fact, this is great. I'm glad. I can't get out of here fast enough."

Before Rob and Billy were out of sight, Tommy began furiously producing his verse on a large piece of cardboard. In bright red letters it blared: "Billy's gone, he don't give a fuck. He called Rob a first-class shmuck."

Pleased with his creative effort, Tommy trotted out to the shop floor and posted the sign in a conspicuous place near the break room.

Moments later Shana, one of the plant's human resources representatives, discovered the sign. Instinct told her not to remove it. She immediately headed for her boss's office. She could see through the window in the door that Margaret was meeting with Billy and Rob. She picked up the intercom and buzzed Margaret.

"Yes," Margaret responded with an irritated tone.

"Margaret, it's Shana. Sorry to interrupt, but I have some critical information dealing with Billy that you need to know now." .

"Yes?" Margaret said, attempting to conceal the nature of the call.

"There's a sign on the shop floor—a poem, probably written by that clown, Tommy." Then Shana repeated the verse for Margaret and waited for instruction.

"That's very interesting. Good work. Call Jess at corporate; he'll instruct you how to handle it. I'll get back with you on this as soon as possible. Thanks for letting me know."

Margaret knew that she would have trouble with this one. The union was strong and would defend to the hilt. Billy was already denying everything Rob alleged he had said. He claimed that Rob was harassing him.

Shana called Jess, the company's corporate labor counsel, and explained the situation. "Do you have a camera, preferably a *Polaroid*?" Jess asked.

"Yes, I think we do."

"When do the breaks begin?"

Shana looked at her watch. "In about forty-five minutes."

"Well, it's important to get out there prior to the break so that no one sees you. Get those pictures pronto. Take two or three, just to make sure they're good ones. And make sure you include something that lets us know it's near the break room. Also, stamp the back of the photos with the time clock. Then give them to Margaret. I'll be in touch."

Shana did as instructed and produced three photos. When she returned to the shop floor later that day, the sign was gone. "Boy, is Jess smart," she thought.

As expected, Billy went directly to the union and grieved the termination, which eventually went to arbitration. Jess flew in from corporate to represent the company at the arbitration. Margaret, Shana, and Rob were also in attendance.

Billy had the union's business agent for his defense and Tommy as a character witness.

Rob began by giving his side of the story, which Billy flatly denied. Then Tommy was called to testify by the business agent.

"Tell me, Tommy," the business agent asked, "how would you describe Billy's work?"

"Excellent, like he's the best. I've learned everything from him," Tommy said.

"How about his interpersonal skills? Does he get along with others?"

"Oh, everyone thinks Billy's the greatest. He's always polite and considerate. I should know; I sit next to him all day long. Like, if he goes for a cup of coffee at break time and it's not convenient for me to pull away at that moment, he offers to bring me back a *Coke*. I mean, he's that kind of guy."

"Have you ever heard Billy argue with anyone or use profanity?"

"No, never. Billy's got three small kids. He's real careful about that sort of thing. He's often told me that he thinks foul language can be as habit-forming as drugs, and he wouldn't consider doing drugs. Nope, not Billy. The guy is just a prince," Tommy expounded sincerely.

"Tell me, Tommy, were you the only other person present when this alleged exchange took place between Rob and Billy?"

"Yes. No one else was there during their discussion," Tommy answered.

"And did you ever hear any part of the conversation that Rob claims took place between them?"

"No way," Tommy lied flawlessly.

"Thank you, Tommy," the business agent responded and turned to Jess. "I have no further questions."

With his opportunity to begin questioning, Jess stood up and slowly moved toward Tommy. "Tell me something, Tommy, is it true that you have a reputation for being the company poet—recording humorous events in the work place?"

"Well, yes," Tommy said, knowing that there was no way to deny his talent.

"Does anyone else in the company do this sort of thing?"

"Nope, only me," Tommy beamed proudly.

"Is it true that your co-workers have asked you to draft up a verse on special occasions—say a retirement party or promotional party?"

"Sure, I do it all the time."

"Does there always have to be a special occasion?"

"Well, no, if I see something humorous, I usually write it up."

"How do you communicate your rhymes to others?"

"Oh, I usually paint them on a big piece of cardboard and put it on the shop floor by the break room to give the guys a laugh when they go for . . ." Tommy had gotten so carried away talking about his talents that by the time he realized what he had done, it was too late.

Jess reached in his pocket, handed Tommy a copy of the verse, and presented another copy to the arbitrator.

"Is this an example of your work found on the shop floor less than thirty minutes after the incident between Rob and Billy?" Jess asked with a clear sense of satisfaction in his tone.

Tommy looked at Billy and sheepishly grinned. "I'm sorry, pal, but they have me."

The arbitrator ruled in favor of the company.

Panel Comments If Rob consistently criticized Billy in front of the other workers, it is not surprising that Billy was insubordinate. This situation looks like a power play. Rob lost a good technician, and Billy lost his job. If Rob had handled this and other problems confidentially, the outcome may have been different.

Legal Comments What about Tommy? He committed perjury by lying under oath in an effort to damage the company's interests and used company equipment for unauthorized purposes. An arbitrator would surely sustain the imposition of some discipline, perhaps even discharge (depending on Tommy's prior work record) for this misconduct.

MINING FOR GOLD

"Those bastards," Sherm griped to his buddy Ron who was standing next to him, "you'd think they could have decent urinals around here. The damn pipes aren't even connected and they leak all over the place." Ron nodded sadly in agreement.

That night Sherm's brother-in-law was over for dinner. "Theo, I have a problem. Maybe you can help me out," Sherm said, passing the potatoes. "We've got crapper problems at our mine facility. The pipes are rusted and leak. The floor is always wet. It's unpleasant as hell. We might as well have an outhouse for all the good our decrepid indoor plumbing does. I've told my supervisor repeatedly about the problem. He says he turns in a report for repairs, but nothing seems to get done. It infuriates me! You work for the county health department, so tell me what I should do."

"File a complaint," Theo commented between chews. "Just give a call and report them. The county inspector will do the rest."

"That's all?" Sherm asked.

"That's all," Theo repeated.

The next morning Sherm was on the phone. He located the Woodfinch County Sanitation Inspector and told him the story. The inspector made a visit that afternoon. Within an hour of the visit, he slapped the company with a health violation and a threat of a hefty fine if repairs were not made within ten days. The company immediately hired a local plumber who completed the job in six days.

Sherm was proud of his accomplishment and bragged to his co-workers that he had made the company tow the line. All the supervisors and managers were equally as happy. They had been requisitioning corporate for months to make a variety of building repairs. It seemed their requests were either denied or ignored. It had been frustrating for everyone concerned.

Unbeknownst to the local management, corporate's reluctance to approve repairs was caused by the knowledge that they were planning to shut down the mine within the next eighteen months. It was an unprofitable business, and they wanted to spend as little as possible on building improvements. The county health department's violation forced them into action.

Despite the decaying office building, the mine had surprisingly well-maintained recreational facilities on the grounds. As part of its reclamation efforts, the company created and stocked several small lakes. Employees frequently spent weekends fishing and camping with their families. The guard at the gate was familiar with all the faces. Most everyone knew everyone else in the town, and most everyone worked at the mine. So it was not surprising when Sherm showed up one weekend.

Instead of going to the lakes, Sherm turned toward the back of the office building. He loaded up his car with welding masks, rods, and other equipment. The guard never noticed Sherm's activities; he was deeply absorbed in his copy of *Field and Stream*. The guard probably never would have noticed—if the squealing of Sherm's back wheels hadn't drawn his attention.

The guard walked around to the back of the building and up to Sherm's car. "What's the trouble here, Sherm? How come your trunk is hanging so low? What do you have in there?"

"Oh, a bunch of company equipment I need for some remodeling I'm doing at home. They gave me permission to borrow it for my project. Damn, I never thought it would be so heavy."

"Well, let's take a look." The guard viewed Sherm's trunk crammed with the equipment.

"And you say you have permission to take this stuff off the premises, Sherm?" the guard asked.

"Yeah, sure . . . uh, Abe Coulton, my supervisor, gave me the okay. You can check with him on Monday."

"Well, I'll do that. In the meantime, let's see if we can get you out of this muck."

The guard attached a winch to Sherm's car and pulled him out of the mud. "That ought to do ya," the guard smiled.

Sherm returned the smile and waved. "Thanks, pal," he said as he drove off.

The guard made a note of the transaction and the type of equipment he saw in the trunk. He placed a note in Abe Coulton's box.

When Abe received the note on Monday morning, he exploded, "What the hell is this noise!" Sherm was already at work down in the mine, but when he emerged for lunch Abe cornered him.

"Sherm, what the hell do you mean, taking company equipment off the premises and telling the guard I gave you permission? Get that stuff back here immediately."

"Sorry, Abe, but I don't have to."

Abe couldn't believe his ears. "Listen, Sherm, you not only have to, if you don't your ass is fired!"

"Fine, go ahead and see what happens," Sherm dared.

Sherm held fast and refused to return the equipment, so Abe processed Sherm's termination and filed a criminal suit against him for theft. Sherm countered with a complaint under the "retaliation provision" of the Mine Safety Help Act. He claimed that the missing equipment was a subterfuge for the real reason for firing him. Sherm contended that his complaint to the county health department about the urinals made management mad, and that's why they fired him.

By the time the case went to court, the company had closed its operations. Nevertheless, corporate was obliged to respond to the suit. Despite management testimony and the best efforts of company attorneys, the company lost the case. Stunned by its loss, the company grimly faced the judgment entitling Sherm to all back pay and related benefits up to the date of closing. Then it dropped its complaint for reimbursement of the stolen welding equipment. At this point, the issue was moot because the welding equipment would have been sold along with all other equipment for pennies on the dollar at the time of closing. So Sherm wound up walking from the courtroom that day receiving thirteen months salary, plus a sizeable inventory of welding equipment—all compliments of the company.

Panel Comments The company should have involved the police at the onset of the incident. If the police had been called immediately, the company would have *at least* recovered its equipment. *At best*, Sherm's successful prosecution would have eliminated the possibility of his winning the appeal over the termination.

Legal Comments While this story is difficult to believe, it does highlight the perils of litigation and the concomitant need for employers to adopt and implement a preventative labor relations policy rather than to be merely reactive.

In many states today, even employees who can be discharged at the employer's will cannot be discharged for reasons that violate public policy (e.g., refusing to lie under oath to conceal illegal company practices) or in retaliation for exercising legal rights (e.g., making safety complaints).

In this case, the employer had a legitimate basis for disciplining the employee for work-related factors (theft and insubordination) wholly unrelated to his exercise of rights (complaining to the health department). So, in theory, the employer had the right to discharge this employee. In reality, however, employers must remember that the question the jury will decide is who to believe— the employee or the company. Because the outcome of the case may hinge on the credibility issue, appropriate documentation is critical, and the company must scrupulously avoid even the appearance of retaliation.

FLAGRANT FELLATIO

"Barbara, there are two gentlemen from the third-shift loading operation here to see you," Nita said. "They seem pretty upset."

"Who are they?"

"One is an older fellow, Carlton Sellers. He's been with us for a long time. The other is Tad Phillips, our purchasing manager's son. Do you want me to pull their files before they come in?"

"No, let's hear what they want first," Barbara said.

Nita escorted the men into Barbara's office. Barbara stood up and extended her hand. "Hi, I'm Barbara Steiner, please have a seat," she offered as she scanned their faces. They each shook her hand in a half-hearted manner. Both looked drained and uncomfortable.

"So how can I help you?" she asked. "You both look quite serious."

Several moments passed in silence. Barbara waited and smiled a warm, encouraging smile. Since neither seemed able to begin, she tried another attempt.

"Obviously this is difficult for you. Let's see if I can help. How many of you worked the third-shift loading operation last night?"

"Fo . . . four of us," Carlton sputtered.

"And who were the other two besides yourself and Tad?"

"Mack, our truck driver, and Ansel, the other loader," Carlton responded.

"Did something unusual happen last night that you want to tell me about?" Barbara coaxed.

Silence again.

"Tad," Barbara began, "how about you? Would you like to offer something?"

Silence.

Barbara's mind raced, "What could have been so horrible that they find it unspeakable? These are two grown men. I'm just going to wait it out until one of them talks." Barbara raised an eyebrow and nodded again in encouragement.

Tad coughed and attempted his turn, "We . . . uh . . . um . . . saw something that we think wasn't right."

"Can you describe what you saw?" Barbara asked.

"Well, maybe we better tell you what led up to it," Carlton interjected.

"Finally, a breakthrough," Barbara thought and then said, "Sure, Carlton, I think that's a good idea."

"Well, Mack drives the truck like we said. And me, Tad, and Ansel load. Well, you see . . . uh . . . um . . . Ansel, he's sort of girly-like, if you know what I mean."

"Go on," Barbara prompted.

"But, Mack—well, he's sorta the opposite. He's a big burly guy who likes to throw his weight around and bully everyone."

"Yeah," Tad chimed in, "we asked him the other day if he brushed his teeth with gun powder, since he's always shooting his mouth off!"

"But this time," Carlton added laughing, "it backfired."

"What do you mean?" Barbara asked, still in the dark.

"Well, he's always teasing Ansel, making comments about his . . . how can I say this delicately?" Tad turned to Carlton looking for help.

"Sexual preference," Carlton suggested.

"Yes, that's it. He's always teasing Ansel about his sexual preference. But, Mack, well, he isn't very delicate. He's anything but. Anyhow, he was going on with normal teasing, and we're just minding our own business loading up the truck when all of a sudden, Mack goes over the deep end."

Silence again.

"The deep end?" Barbara assisted.

"Well, he . . . um . . . ma'am, I don't know if I can say this in front of a lady," Tad said as his face flushed crimson.

"It's okay," Barbara assured him, "I won't get angry with you or be offended."

"Well, okay, here goes." Tad took a deep breath and unloaded his words with machine gun speed, "Out of the blue, Mack yells to Ansel across the floor, 'Hey, faggot, why don't you suck my cock?' So Ansel drops the package he was carrying, takes a running start, drops to his knees, and slides for the next ten feet until he stops smack dab in front of Mack. Then he unzips Mack's pants, pulls it out, and puts it in his mouth."

"And then what did you do?" Barbara asked, trying not to act horrified.

"We didn't do nothing," Carlton added. "We were too shocked. We just kept loading. As a matter of fact, we couldn't even talk to each other until our shift was over. That's when we decided to come to you."

"Well, I'm certainly glad you did," Barbara said. "I know this was difficult for you to discuss, but I appreciate your efforts. We will look into this immediately. In the meantime, is there anything else I need to know?"

Carlton and Tad looked at each other and shrugged. "I guess not. That's it," Carlton said.

The next evening Barbara and other key management stayed for the third shift operation and called in Ansel and Mack. Confronted with the evidence, both men denied everything. Despite their denials, the two were fired. Ansel threatened to picket the company for discriminating against gays, but he never followed through. Mack, on the other hand, had another agenda.

The company filed a report to the state unemployment office. They indicated that the reason for termination was "public participation in a homosexual activity." Although this was considered a misdemeanor according to state law, the company could not contest the men's application for benefits. Interestingly, in the state in which this occurred, a misdemeanor was not a basis for denial of unemployment.

Mack contended, however, that the information about homosexual activities in the company's report to the unemployment office labeled him a homosexual and constituted defamation. Thus, he hired a hungry young lawyer on contingency to pursue this position. The attorney then sent a letter to the corporation demanding reinstatement and a settlement of $300,000 in damages. Corporate labor counsel recognized this frivolous claim as a feeble attempt by Mack's greedy young lawyer to legally extort money. So when Mack's lawyer threatened a lawsuit if the company didn't settle, labor counsel didn't flinch and welcomed the battle. Mack pursued arbitration under the existing labor contract and was badly beaten. Then the corporation's insurance company whipped him again on the civil law suit under summary judgment. With Carlton and Tad's excellent testimony, Mack not only had to relive the embarrassment twice over but also lost both his cases as well.

Barbara should have obtained contemporaneous written statements from Carlton and Tad. **Legal Comments** As "Perverse Verse" demonstrates, employees often change their version of the events when the time comes to testify against a co-worker.

With respect to Mack's defamation suit, truth is always a valid defense to a defamation claim, so it is not surprising that Mack lost.

Finally, an employer's statements made in the course of an unemployment compensation proceeding will almost never subject the employer to liability, so long as these statements are relevant to the claim, factual, and not malicious. In legal parlance, an employer's statement of reasons for dismissing an employee in response to a claim for unemployment benefits is "privileged." In order to reduce the risk of a libel suit, the company documentation should have been a descriptive account of the actual behaviors (e.g., engaged in oral sex) rather than a characterization of them (e.g., participated in a homosexual activity).

12
ROGUES
AND
DESPERADOS

A subculture of scoundrels may flourish for years without a company's knowledge. They strike deals, commit illegal acts, and profit without regard for laws or mores. Some of these rogues will go to any extreme to settle a grudge or obtain satisfaction. Usually, we don't find out about their plans until one of their schemes backfires. And then, whether we like it or not, we're fully immersed! The scariest part is that we have no way to predict what, where, or when things will explode or who will get hurt. Our best defense is to develop good, solid detective skills: observe carefully, listen closely, and trust your instincts.

A DEADLY DEAL

Mandy fidgeted with her key ring while she waited for Rex Hartly, the director of security, to arrive. When Rex walked in the reception area, Mandy leapt from her seat and blocked his path. "Mr. Hartly, Mr. Hartly, can I see you? Please, I know I don't have an appointment, but I don't have much time. It's very important!" she pleaded.

"Of course, that's what we're here for," he assured her, calmly ushering her to his office.

"Well, Mr. Hartly, I don't know exactly how to begin, but I'm in serious trouble."

"How about beginning with your name?" he smiled.

Mandy blushed. "Oh, I'm sorry. I'm Amanda Barleycorn, but you can call me Mandy—everyone does. I work second shift on the welding line."

"Okay, Mandy, what's bothering you?"

"Can I be assured you won't involve the police?" she asked.

"I can't promise you that, Mandy," he responded. "If you've committed a serious crime, it's my responsibility to report it. I'll try to help in any way that I can, though."

"Well, I don't suppose I have any choice. I almost committed a crime. Well, actually I'm trying to stop a crime I was going to commit. God, this is hard to talk about."

Rex had no idea what her problem was. He tried another tactic.

"Mandy, what crime are you trying to stop?"

"A hit on my husband," she gulped.

"You mean you are trying to have your husband killed?"

"*Was trying*—those are the operative words. I chickened out. I changed my mind. Joe and I made up. He's getting counseling and isn't hittin' me anymore."

"So, how did you stop it?"

"I told you, he's getting counseling."

"No, Mandy, I mean how did you stop the contract on your husband," Rex clarified.

"I told him not to do it—to call it off."

"So, did the hit man agree?"

"No, not exactly."

"What do you mean?"

"There's more to it."

"Go on," Rex said, thinking, "I hope this ditzy lady can get to the point. I'm starting to lose my patience."

"Well, you see, I became friendly with Johnny Fletcher, who works third shift in wiring. And well, he'd always hang out a couple hours early, so we met during break time. Anyhow, we got to talkin', and I was telling him about my problems with Joe—that's my husband, see. I was just wishin' Joe out of my life, when Johnny said he could do it for me. I asked how, and he said that he could sorta be my broker."

"A broker?"

"Yeah, sort of a go-between. He said he knew a guy . . . who, you know . . . knew a guy who was a professional shooter. The kind that didn't make 'em suffer. Just got 'em on the first pop. Anyhow, Johnny said the shooter was out of town, but he could make arrangements. I just needed to give him a down payment."

"Did you give Johnny the money?"

"Yes, it sounded good at the time."

"All of it?"

"No, only the down payment. That's where things start gettin' kinda sticky. See . . . well . . . uh . . . . Wait a minute. Let me back up. I changed my mind, so I told Johnny the deal was off. Then Johnny said that finding the shooter cost him some money, and he wanted to be paid whether the job was done or not. I said, 'No way.' Then he threatened me that he'd tell everyone at work what I was up to if I didn't pay up the balance. Then I told him that was extortion, and extortion was illegal. But Johnny doesn't seem to think so, and he keeps hounding me. Well, I'm sick of it. So, I just figured, I might as well tell on myself and beat him to the punch. No telling how he might make more of the story than was true."

"Has Johnny threatened you in any other way?" Rex asked.

"No, not really, but do you think you can get him off my back?"

"I'm not sure. I'm not even sure any crime has been committed. Let me do some investigation, and I'll get back to you."

Rex met with Johnny when he arrived for his shift. He presented Mandy's story to him and asked him if it was true. Johnny, as Rex suspected, denied everything.

With Mandy's disclosure, it was unlikely that Johnny had anything further with which to threaten her. It was also unlikely that Johnny would arrange to carry out the hit on Mandy's husband because she hadn't given him enough money. Besides, if something did happen to her husband, Johnny had already been implicated. Since Mandy's change of heart prevented the crime from taking place, there seemed no real reason to involve the police, so Rex closed the case. Both Johnny and Mandy remained employed by the company and continued to work without further incident.

Panel Comments Sometimes you wish you hadn't parked so far from the guard shack! As more stories of employee rampages at their place of employment are covered in the news, people begin to question the safety of the work place. Employer liability in terms of what they "should have known might happen" are forcing businesses to anticipate new ways to protect their workers. In this case, Rex should have investigated the matter further and documented his findings in Mandy's file.

Just because this turned out all right doesn't mean that Johnny wasn't extorting from others or behaving inappropriately toward the company in other matters. We would be very concerned about both of these people's honesty and judgment as workers.

Legal Comments Rex's decision that "there seemed to be no real reason to involve the police" is questionable. It is rarely correct for a manager to decide unilaterally whether or not criminal activity occurred. That is a question for the police. At a minimum, the company should obtain the advice of competent criminal defense counsel before deciding what to do. Indeed, Rex or the company may have liability for failing to report known criminal activity. And should the "hit" actually take place, Rex and the company's failure to act could be disastrous for them (not to mention the hittee). Finally, allowing Johnny and Mandy to continue to be employed appears to be inviting trouble. Their participation in a palpably criminal conspiracy would almost surely be a sufficient ground to terminate them.

AN ELABORATE EXTORTION

Sara Blaisdel was one of the brightest, most respected human resources professionals in the country. She held dual masters degrees, one in criminology and the other in industrial relations. Because of her background, the corporation's Human Resources and Security Departments were under her domain. Although she had an unusually high batting average for solving cases, they were nothing like the one she was about to face. Sara's most exciting challenge came the day the chief executive officer called her in to meet with Special Agent Tanner from the FBI.

Both men were standing when she entered the room. "Sara," Morgan Fuller began, "I'd like you to meet Special Agent Rick Tanner from the Federal Bureau of Investigation."

Chills ran up Sara's spine. She felt electricity in the air. This had to be a big one. She nodded and extended her hand. Agent Tanner grasped her hand firmly as they greeted each other with a professional handshake.

"Please, let's all take seat," Morgan said in a serious tone. "Sara, we received an extortion letter in the mail yesterday. As you know, any threat to a financial institution engaged in interstate commerce violates the Hobbs Act, so I immediately contacted Special Agent Tanner. I've told him about your background and that you'd cooperate with him during the investigation. He suspects the extortionist is an employee or a customer. Although he has some ideas on how to begin, he's also interested in your thoughts."

"May I see the letter?" Sara asked.

"Certainly, here's a copy," Morgan responded.

Sara reviewed the letter.

Mr. Fuller:

Your company has never treated people right. I'm tired of dealing with you and all your bureaucratic nonsense. The last dealing I had with you was the final straw, and you're going to pay for all the trouble and stress you've caused me if you don't do as I ask.

I've listed my demands, warnings, and instructions as follows:

DEMANDS
- *$250,000 in unmarked bills, not to exceed $50 denominations.*
- *Place these bills in a leather briefcase.*

INSTRUCTIONS
- *Rent a red Jeep Cherokee.*
- *On March 10, at 5:45 A.M., drive the Jeep to the corner of Billings and Cooper Streets. You will find a note wedged in the telephone pole in a spot five feet from the ground. This note will tell you where to go for your next instruction.*
- *Follow each and every instruction thereafter.*

WARNINGS
- *Do not involve the police.*
- *Do not attempt to follow your courier.*
- *Do not depart from my instructions in the slightest.*
- *Do not attempt to remove the note earlier than the appointed time.*

If you do not respond to my request exactly as I have stated, I will do severe damage to each of your facilities. Each week, one by one, I will damage them, until you fulfill my demands.

Sara looked up. "What are you planning to do?"

"We are going to take the writer seriously," Agent Tanner responded. "We've got to go along with his game and, in the interim, try to figure out who he or she might be—although I do suspect it's a *he*. Today is March 8, so we only have two days to prepare. I already have agents working around the clock. They're staking out the corner in hopes of catching him when he plants the note. Chances are the note is there already, but we don't want to make any assumptions. Another agent, Jack Mills, and I will deliver the money, but Mills won't be visible in the vehicle."

"Why do you suppose he was so specific about the type of car?" Sara asked and then answered her own question. "Do you think he intends to take you on some back roads that are not paved?"

"Precisely," Agent Tanner responded. "I wouldn't be surprised if he takes us off the road into a deeply-wooded area."

"I suggest we focus our effort in two places," Sara began. "I think we need to get Mel Hardin from Consumer Affairs involved. We need to determine who has filed complaints against the company and look for multiple complaints. At the same time, I'm going to run a list of employees who have recently separated from the company for any purpose—whether discharged, quit, or retired—during the past three years. Then we'll scan the exit interviews on these employees to determine if any of them expressed dissatisfaction in any area."

"What do you estimate is the number of employees who have separated from the organization in the past three years?" Tanner asked.

"We went through a major downsizing last year. So, including all our subsidiaries, we probably have 1,900 to 2,100. I know that seems like an inordinately high number, but our records are computerized. We have a code that indicates dissatisfaction. When we run a search, we'll probably be able to bring that number down to three hundred records. Then we can easily scan the reasons. Many of them are very minor. We'll pull out those with the most severe dissatisfaction.. That should take us down to about a hundred. Then I'll look at the most recent files first. I'll break them down into groups of ten and attack them," she responded eagerly.

"Excellent approach," Agent Tanner agreed. "I'll send over two of our best agents to assist you when you're ready."

"Terrific," Sara said, "but we'll need some help in consumer affairs as well."

"No problem," Agent Tanner indicated. "After you've briefed Mel Hardin, let us know the volume, and we'll supply the manpower."

"Great," she confirmed and stood up.

Morgan Fuller was glad to know that things were being handled by a competent staff, but he was still very worried about the whole mess. He attempted to mask his feelings when he said, "Thanks, Sara, keep me posted. If this madman is an employee, I have every confidence you'll flush him out."

"We will, don't worry, Morgan," she assured him, sensing his grave concern.

Sara left Morgan's office and picked up the phone in the reception room. "Mel," she said, "it's Sara. We've got an emergency. Can I see you now?"

"Of course," Mel responded.

"I'm on my way," she clicked off.

Sara arrived at Mel's office and showed him the letter. She instructed him what to look for and gave him Agent Tanner's number to ask for assistance. Mel promised to call him and get right on the investigation.

Sara left Mel's office and called her staff assistant, Mark Engle, for a briefing. Mark was a wizard with the PC and delivered the report she requested in less than an hour. She reviewed the exit interview report, which identified the individual reasons for each employee's dissatisfaction. Within an hour she had checked off 125 names and asked Mark to pull the files. She also asked him to arrange them in chronological order by most recent date of separation.

It was relatively easy to get the files pulled, since Mark recruited a half dozen helpers. The files were stacked in her office, ordered chronologically, within an hour and a half.

Sara dialed Agent Tanner. "Agent Tanner?"

"Yes, this is Agent Tanner," he responded.

"This is Sara Blaisdel. I have the files. When can you send over your troops?"

"You have the files pulled already?"

"Yep," she answered, pleased that she had been able to produce such speedy action.

"It's two o'clock now. I'll have them work on this through the night. They'll be there before 4:00 P.M. By the way, good work, Sara."

"Thanks, Agent Tanner."

"Please, call me Rick."

"Fine, Rick. I'll look forward to working with them."

Sara stared at the stacks of files. "Might as well pull off my first set of ten," she said to herself, slicing off a pile. The first file was Eleanor Houston. Eleanor complained that her supervisor was unfair about vacation schedules and work distribution. She claimed that she was tired of getting all the hard assignments and being overburdened. She also said the pay was low. Eleanor had found a job working as a school secretary. She liked the hours and free parking. Eleanor had worked for the company for two years and had no other documents in her file.

"This one's a 'no,'" Sara determined. She closed the file and dropped it on the floor. "Let's see who's next—Sheila Laudert. What was her major beef?" Sara said to herself.

"Claimed her co-workers discriminated against her because she was fat. They excluded her from all activities and made fun of her. She complained to the supervisor who did nothing. She also stated that even though her performance ratings were good, she was held back for promotion. Said the company should have provided her with wider chairs and wider aisles. She couldn't take it any longer. She found a job with a hospital. Sheila was married with two children," Sara read to herself.

"Nope, not likely," Sara thought, when she noticed that Sheila had short-term stints with all her previous employers. "She's probably had this happen many times over. No reason to expect she would target us for her hit. Besides, she doesn't seem aggressive enough." Sara dropped the file and opened the next one.

"Benton Jarvis," Sara read on the label. "Boy, this is a thick file. Let's see . . . took the 'fifty-five and out' special early retirement deal. It says here that he felt he was basically forced into retirement after twenty-five years of service. He claims the early retirement program was a sham to get him out. He thought the company's performance appraisal was biased and unfair. He should not be held to standards. He didn't feel his performance should be measured. Said his career was thwarted by the company because he was continually passed over for promotions."

"Hmm . . . this is a 'maybe,'" Sara thought. "Long-term resentment building up. Could be some real rage festering here." She tapped her pencil on her chin and tried to recollect if she had ever met him personally. She hadn't, and looked back down at his file. "Let's see what else is here. Oh my gosh!" she exclaimed aloud as she saw the first letter he had written contesting a health benefit. She flipped further through the papers. "I can't believe this," she said when she found a second and third letter of complaint about a company policy.

Each letter was written in exactly the same style as the extortion letter. Each letter stated the problem and contained topic headings and indented bullets to state the points that followed. "This is our guy, I just know it!"

She called up the vice president of claims. "Norman, this Sara Blaisdel in Human Resources. I need a favor, and I need it immediately. Please find out if we insure Benton Jarvis for auto or homeowners. If we do, I need copies of his claim files ASAP. Can you help me?"

"Can you tell me what this is about?" Norman asked.

"Sorry, Norm, I can't. But the request comes from the top. I know I can count on your nondisclosure."

"Of course, Sara, I'll request it immediately and have my assistant hand deliver it to you."

"Thanks, Norm. You're wonderful."

Sara couldn't wait to get her hands on those files. She knew all she had was circumstantial evidence, but instinct told her that there would be other clues. She didn't know what they were exactly, but she knew they would be important.

At 4:55 P.M. Norm's assistant delivered the file. Sara was beside herself with excitement. "The hunt is on," she thought as she dug through the files.

Jarvis's auto file revealed he owned two vehicles, a *Honda Accord* and a four-wheel drive *Ford Bronco*. "Damn, I can't believe this, a *Bronco* . . ." Sara was literally bouncing in her chair at this point. Then she attacked the homeowner's file. "Nothing unusual in the past few years," she thought with disappointment. "Wait . . . oh my gosh . . . he owns guns."

The file indicated that a shotgun was stolen, and Jarvis had submitted a bill for a replacement. "Let's see this bill is from Sizemore's Gun Shop, Portsmouth, Maine. Oh, I don't know," she deliberated. "He could just be a hunter, but I better note the place where he bought his gun and the serial number," she decided and summarized her information.

She and the other agents went through the rest of the files that evening and the next day. Benton Jarvis remained the number one suspect. In the meantime, Special Agents Tanner and Mills prepared to pick up the extortionist note at the appointed time from the telephone pole on the corner of Billings and Cooper. Tanner emerged from the car and located the pole. The note was exactly where the extortionist had indicated, carefully protected in a sealed plastic bag.

Drive to Henderson's Pharmacy on Nilan Avenue. There is a soda fountain in the back. Your next instruction will be attached under the counter at the third stool from the left.

Tanner came back to the jeep and informed Mills of the next stop. When they arrived at Henderson's Pharmacy, a brown envelope was affixed to the underside of the counter. *Pick up your next instructions at the phone booth at the Newport exit off I-95.*

This was a two-hour drive and the pair continued on their journey. They found the next set of instructions at the phone booth. *Go to the rear of the grocery mart in Blue Hill. Look in the rear of the dumpster.*

It was another two-hour drive to Blue Hill. The dumpster had the last message, which contained a map of a secluded area about fifty miles away. The map pointed to a creek and a pasture with a lone tree. They were to put the briefcase by the tree in the pasture and leave.

By the time the two arrived, it had grown dark. Mills waited hidden in the jeep while Tanner emerged from the vehicle with the briefcase in his hand. As Tanner stepped a few feet away from the jeep, a shot echoed and splintered Tanner's leg. Mills flashed a large floodlight in the direction of the shot.

"FBI, drop your weapon!" Mills demanded.

The gunman emptied his shotgun into the jeep's front tires, dropped his gun, and escaped on foot. Mills radioed for help and a helicopter flew in to assist. That evening agents swarmed the area. They couldn't find the gunman, but they located his shotgun.

Sara hardly slept that night. She had hoped to hear something before leaving work that day, but Tanner had not called. The next day she called the chief executive officer first thing for an update. Morgan informed her of the prior day's events. When he told her about Tanner, she interrupted.

"Is Tanner okay?" she asked, shaken by the news.

"Yes, he's fine, though his doctor says he'll be in a cast for awhile."

"Oh, God, this guy is really serious. We've got to find him!" she said.

"They found Jarvis's gun," Morgan commented.

"His gun? What kind of gun? Did they tell you what type?"

"I don't know."

"Morgan, I've got to talk to Tanner . . . or his partner. Right now."

"Fine, they're still in Maine. Here's the number."

Sara spoke to Mills and filled him in on her suspect. She told him about the gunsmith in Portsmouth, where Benton had purchased his new shotgun. She gave him the serial numbers.

Mills paid a visit to the gunsmith. The gunsmith checked the serial number and matched them to Benton. He recalled having made recent repairs to the very same gun, and his records reflected a match to the serial number.

Benton didn't elude the agents for long. They tracked him down at his sister's house in Vermont. When they arrived, he appeared dejected and confused. Benton was later tried and convicted under the Hobbs Act. Currently, he's serving out his term in a federal corrections facility.

Panel Comments For a secret investigation that could involve insiders, too many people were involved in the research. Also, Sara should have advised the agent of the gun information as soon as she became aware.

Legal Comments In favorable contrast to some other cases throughout the book, here the company made a prudent decision to involve and cooperate with the police. In cases where potential criminal conduct is involved, companies should avoid playing the role of prosecuting attorney, judge, or jury.

EPILOGUE

Do you have a story to equal or top these? If you do and would like to share it with me, please copy this page, sign and complete the form, and send it off to me. If I decide to produce a sequel, I'll contact you by mid-1992 to begin my research.

RELEASE

I would like to schedule an interview with Elizabeth Fried to provide her information for a book which she intends to publish. I understand that names, locations, and other pertinent organizational information will be changed.

I am voluntarily participating in Elizabeth's project and do not expect to be paid in any way for having told Elizabeth these anecdotes. I also understand she is free to communicate this information in her own literary style and to exercise editorial license as she or her publisher deems necessary. I promise I will disclose to no one else that I have discussed the facts and circumstances of these anecdotes with Elizabeth Fried or that I am aware that any published accounting of the facts and circumstances of these anecdotes will be made by her.

I represent that I am personally familiar with the facts and circumstances of these anecdotes and that everything I relate is true to the best of my knowledge.

_____   _____
Signature   Date

Please print the following and mail a copy to:
    Ms. Elizabeth Fried, Ph.D.
    President
    N. E. Fried and Associates, Inc.
    5590 Dumfries Court West, Ste. 1900
    Dublin, OH 43017-9436

Name:_____

Company:_____

Work Phone:_____ Home Phone:_____

Years of Human Resources Experience _____

Years of Supervisory Experience _____

ABOUT THE AUTHOR

N. Elizabeth Fried is president of N. E. Fried and Associates, Inc., a national management consulting firm, located in Dublin, Ohio. The firm, which was established in 1983, specializes in salary management, short-term incentive plans, and sales compensation. The firm serves clients ranging from small, entrepreneurial businesses to Fortune 500 companies.

Elizabeth received her Ph.D. from The Ohio State University and her Certified Compensation Professional Designation from the American Compensation Association (ACA). Additionally, she is listed in *Who's Who of American Women* and *Who's Who of Emerging Leaders in America.* A vibrant and entertaining speaker, she regularly addresses professional and business groups on a variety of human resources topics.

Elizabeth conducts compensation research on a national scale and has been quoted widely in such publications as *The Wall Street Journal, Chicago Tribune, Washington Post, Commerce Clearinghouse, Bureau of Business Practices,* and *Bureau of National Affairs.* A prolific writer, she is frequently invited to contribute to professional journals and trade publications, which feature her research on secretarial grading practices and compensation arrangements designed to retain key people during acquisitions, mergers, and divestitures. She has written for ACA's *Technical Perspectives in Compensation, HR Magazine, Journal of Compensation and Benefits, Journal of Staffing and Recruitment, Prentice Hall Compensation Service, Maxwell Macmillan,* and *Human Resource Executive.*

Elizabeth currently teaches two certification seminars for ACA, one on quantitative analysis and the other on job analysis, job evaluation, and job description writing. She also served as adjunct faculty at Franklin University from 1979 to 1986, where she taught a comprehensive course in wage and salary administration.

Outrageous Conduct: Bizarre Behavior at Work is her first creative work. Additional copies may be ordered from the Society for Human Resource Management, 606 N. Washington St., Alexandria VA 22314. 1-800-444-5006.

Elizabeth Fried is available as a keynote speaker for management and professional meetings and conventions. Please contact Alexandra Fuller at 614-766-9800 for scheduling and fee arrangements.